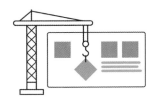

A Trainer's Guide to PowerPoint

BEST PRACTICES FOR MASTER PRESENTERS

Mike Parkinson

atd PRESS

A Trainer's Guide to PowerPoint: Best Practices for Master Presenters is an independent publication and is neither affiliated with, nor authorized, sponsored, or approved by, Microsoft Corporation.

Adobe product screenshot(s) reprinted with permission from Adobe Systems Incorporated.

ATD Press is an internationally renowned source of insightful and practical information on talent development, training, and professional development.

ATD Press
1640 King Street
Alexandria, VA 22314 USA

Ordering information: Books published by ATD Press can be purchased by visiting ATD's website at www.td.org/books or by calling 800.628.2783 or 703.683.8100.

Library of Congress Control Number: 2018939596

ISBN-10: 1-947308-52-1
ISBN-13: 978-1-947308-52-7
e-ISBN: 978-1-947308-53-4

ATD Press Editorial Staff
Director: Kristine Luecker
Manager: Melissa Jones
Community of Practice Manager, Learning Technologies: Justin Brusino
Developmental Editor: Kathryn Stafford
Senior Associate Editor: Caroline Coppel
Text Design: Jason Mann and Iris Sanchez
Cover Design: Derek Thornton, Faceout

Printed by Versa Press, East Peoria, IL

Contents

Introduction 1

Phase 1: Discover 11
    Chapter 1: The Four Keys to Discovery:
    Problem, Mission, Learner, and Subject Matter 13

Phase 2: Design 35
    Chapter 2: Writing a Powerful Takeaway 37
    Chapter 3: Storyboards for Faster Design 49
    Chapter 4: Render: PowerPoint Tips, Tricks, and Secrets 67
    Chapter 5: Render: Design Principles for Professional Slides 99

Phase 3: Deliver 127
    Chapter 6: 10 Best PowerPoint Delivery Practices 129
    Chapter 7: Delivering Your PowerPoint Presentation 143

Afterword 157
Appendix A 159
Appendix B 171
Glossary 175
References 183
About the Author 185
Index 187

Introduction

I f I gave you a paintbrush and paint, could you paint a masterpiece?

Most likely you couldn't, unless you were a trained artist.

Just like a paintbrush and paint, Microsoft PowerPoint is a tool. The tool doesn't make the art; you do, through your skill and talent. Learning how to use PowerPoint is the secret to making effective presentations and learning materials.

PowerPoint epitomizes the term *ubiquitous*. The number of PowerPoint users is mind-blowing—even if the only available data are outdated. Robert Gaskins (n.d.), the founder of PowerPoint, wrote that in 2003, more than 500 million PowerPoint users worldwide were making more than 30 million presentations every day. These numbers are still widely circulated and have not been updated, but that equates to well over 10 billion presentations annually. On average, PowerPoint is used more than 350 times per second (PowerPointInfo 2017). Even if the actual numbers were half this estimate, PowerPoint eclipses the use of all other similar tools combined. Wherever you find a computer, you will likely find a PowerPoint user.

Having so many PowerPoint users at different skill levels creates a reoccurring challenge—lack of quality and effectiveness. Feedback for PowerPoint presentations range from "What was the point?" to "That changed my life." Unfortunately, most fall closer to the former reaction.

What are the key traits of a powerful, effective PowerPoint presentation? I have identified six:

1. engaging throughout
2. professional
3. clearly connects the dots between the learner, the objectives, and the content
4. easy to understand
5. easy to remember
6. easy to apply.

How many presentations have you seen that achieve these benchmarks—100, 20, 10, none? Compare your number with the total number of presentations you have seen. I'm guessing the amount of successful educational presentations is relatively low.

The reason we don't encounter better PowerPoint presentations is because most presenters don't know how to create them. That is why I wrote this book and, I assume, why you are reading it. I want to share with you how to effectively use PowerPoint and reveal what the best-of-the-best PowerPoint designers and presenters do.

PowerPoint is an amazing tool. It offers a variety of features that align with the needs of presenters in every industry. The software is many things to many people; it isn't always used for one purpose. Trainers and facilitators can use it to make presentations, graphics, storyboards, handouts, brochures, and more.

However, PowerPoint's default settings and built-in functionality do not always encourage best practices; its features can lead users astray. For example, bullets are a key part of PowerPoint's standard settings. In a presentation, bullets are better than paragraphs of text, but they are usually unnecessary. They often act more as speaker notes than training elements.

When most presenters start using PowerPoint, they focus on the default features and "gee-wiz" effects like WordArt (Figure I-1).

Figure I-1. PowerPoint Default WordArt Features

The result is an unprofessional presentation that looks like every other unsuccessful presentation. Explaining what functionality to use or avoid is not enough to become a PowerPoint expert. That's like showing someone how to operate a camera and expecting an Ansel Adams photograph. It's more than knowing what to do; it's knowing why to do it.

Take something as simple as choosing the colors for your presentation. Knowing how to change your PowerPoint's theme colors is much easier than knowing which colors to choose to get optimal results. Do you choose colors you like? Do you select hues from an online color picker? Do you base your palette on your organization's brand? Knowing why you choose which colors is much more important than knowing how to change them in PowerPoint.

This book focuses on developing professional, powerful PowerPoint presentations that improve understanding, recollection, and adoption. There is no magic button to make awesome slides. However, there are proven processes and tools that deliver successful PowerPoint content every time you use them. For example, PowerPoint is not a graphics package, but it can be used to build amazing graphics—if you know how.

The formal steps in this book are intended to give you a solid, repeatable approach to presentation design. There is no one-size-fits-all process for making successful PowerPoint presentations and educational materials. As you gain more experience, some steps will become intuitive, and you will not always need to doggedly follow the exact method. You will learn the best practices and tailor them to meet your specific needs.

To learn this process, we must first define and agree on key terminology. When I refer to the presenter, I mean the person or organization sharing the PowerPoint material. *Author* means the person (or people) in charge of developing the presentation (and learning materials). *Audience* and *target audience* denote the learners intended to receive your content. *Conceptualize* refers to the process of creating a design or design plan. It often involves visualizing and graphically representing your content.

The process shown in this book is founded on two principal needs. Selecting the right PowerPoint features to meet your learners' goals is easy when you know what functions or approaches elicit what responses. The process shown in this book is founded on two principal needs.

Two Principal Needs

When cultivating and growing skills through training, there are two principal needs you must keep in mind:

1. Communicate the necessary information in a way that is easily understood and applied.
2. Engage the learner.

Aside from presentations used for pure statistical analysis of empirical data (in which case, use a better-suited tool), almost all PowerPoint presentations are meant to engage our audience and improve learning. How to engage the learner is based on a combination of understanding basic human behavior and knowing what motivates them.

A successful presentation answers your audience's questions. It tells the learner who, what, where, when, why, and how. The content makes it easy for the learner to go from attending a PowerPoint-based seminar to achieving all learning objectives.

How Learners Learn

How we learn is the foundation on which you build content. Knowing how to improve understanding, recollection, and adoption is key. Don't swim against the current; use your audience's natural brain functions to your advantage.

To make successful presentations and learning materials, you need to recognize the two levels of audience communication—conscious (intellectual) and unconscious (emotional):

- **Conscious communication** is the intellectual, analytical, and surface processes involved in comprehending the information presented. It is the presentation's (and the presenter's) ability to communicate content in a way that is easy to intellectually digest. It is the information your audience knowingly processes. I call it surface communication. For example, think of the last time you attended a presentation. When you studied the slides, you made a conscious choice to engage with and interpret the content. It is what you chose to focus on—to read and hear. One of the conscious mind's jobs is to keep our unconscious mind on the right path. Both your conscious and unconscious mind create checks and balances to make sure you stay on the right path.

- **Unconscious communication** is the emotional effect the presented materials have on your learners' state of mind. It influences whether they are truly engaged and can easily recall the content shared. Everything we take in elicits an emotional response—whether we know it or not. Successful PowerPoint content harnesses this aspect of the human mind to influence and motivate audiences. For example, you could use pictures of tragic accidents to provoke your audience to change their driving behavior by emotionally connecting what they are learning to an undesirable outcome. Color choice alone is shown to sway your learners' moods.

Research is proving that the vast majority of our choices and actions depend upon brain activity that is outside our conscious awareness (Ariely 2010; Bargh 2007). Based on my observations and reading, I (nonscientifically) estimate that 95 percent of learning and the application of what we learn is subconscious (Figure I-2). For example, do you need to concentrate to breathe, blink, walk, talk, write, type, or tie your shoes? Have you learned something simply by watching others? Have you thought, "I don't like the look of that?" That's because our unconscious mind is constantly learning, making quick decisions, and applying what we learn while our conscious mind goes on to other tasks. In many situations, the unconscious mind can actually outperform the conscious mind (Dijksterhuis 2009). Even life-and-death activities are governed by our unconscious mind. For example, something as dangerous as driving is supposed to be a conscious, focused activity, but while you were driving, have you ever wondered, "Where am I? Did I miss my turn?" Most of what we do in life—even driving—is unconscious.

I regularly conduct an experiment in my workshops. I ask for a volunteer who drives. I hand the person a paper plate and say, "This your vehicle's steering wheel. Can you show us how you change lanes from the center lane to the right lane? You've already turned on your blinker, and checked your mirrors and blind spots. We just don't know what you do with the steering wheel." To date, no one has correctly showed how to turn the wheel to change lanes. Volunteers forget that after turning the wheel right to move into the right lane, you then have to turn your wheel back to the left to straighten your car's tires and continue moving forward. Of course, they know how to do it—unconsciously. They do it almost every day. The issue is that most of our actions are driven (no pun intended) by a powerful part of our brain.

Figure I-2. The Relationship Between the Unconscious Mind and the Conscious Mind

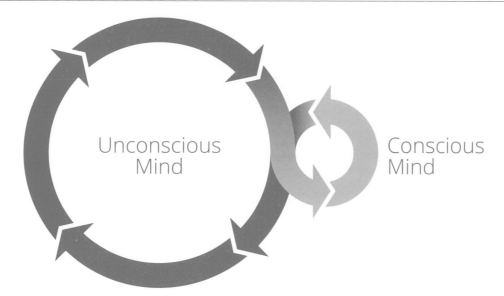

Conscious and unconscious communications are interrelated; each affects the other. For example, do you make a habit of buying from people you don't trust? Trust is an amalgamation of analytical and emotional observations and conclusions. The same is true with how participants see and choose. All surface and subsurface inputs interact to form a cohesive picture of the content for your learners. Assuming no other input, what your audience sees and hears combine to create the lasting impression of the presenter and ultimately leads to a positive or negative end result.

In his 2006 book, *The Happiness Hypothesis,* psychologist Jonathan Haidt uses a fantastic metaphor to understand the relationship between the two parts of our brain. He wrote that the emotional, automatic side is an elephant, and the analytical, controlled side is its rider (Figure I-3). The rational rider's job is to maintain control when the irrational elephant wants to leave the path.

Figure I-3. The Emotional and Analytical Sides of the Human Brain

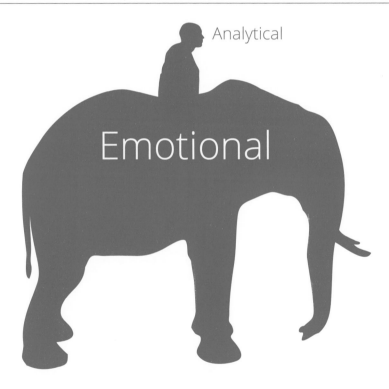

When we process information, our unconscious mind is constantly working—largely without our awareness or supervision. The benefit is often that we learn important stuff faster, have fun, stay safe, and stay alive (that is, it regulates automatic body functions). It even helps us solve problems over time. How often has a solution popped into your mind while you were in the shower or falling asleep?

Unconscious thought is a part of all decision making and almost always trumps the conscious mind. Ignoring this impedes learning. For example, if you want your presentation to be seen as professional and compelling, then every aspect must be consistent with that desire. If your presentation is aesthetically unappealing and riddled with grammatical errors, your audience will question the quality of the content being shared. The incongruence of the conscious and unconscious communication confuses learners' minds. Your audience begins to doubt that the presentation is worth their attention. The "elephant" will likely leave the path.

Your participants are bombarded with competing information. There is too much to consciously process, so your learners take shortcuts. Their brains quickly determine if it is worth their time and use brain tricks to acquire knowledge. We want to tap into that. For example, when I teach participants how to render PowerPoint infographics, I include step-by-step instructions. Learners quickly decide that they want to make professional graphics like the ones they see, and I show them (along with accompanying text) how to do it themselves. The images act as a brain cheat sheet—a quick reference guide. I'm tapping into how the brain learns best.

As trainers and facilitators, it is in our best interest to tap into unconscious learning and application to improve the outcome for our audience.

Because everything we absorb elicits an emotional response that affects our state of mind, your presentation will also communicate other, less identifiable, unconscious ideas, such as the credibility, competency, professionalism, reliability, creativity, and strength of the presenter. Your goal is to elicit emotions in your audience that support the author's and presenter's goals.

Knowing how to involve both the conscious and unconscious mind is a secret that great trainers and facilitators use. If you follow the methodology laid out in this book, you will too.

> According to neurologist and Nobel Laureate Eric Kandel, it is easier to repress cognitive experiences than it is to repress emotional (unconscious) experiences.
>
> —Kruglinski (2006)

The Process

Using a process to make successful PowerPoint presentations gives repeatable, predictable results. It supports the two principal needs and relies on how participants really learn. The process I'm sharing is arranged into three phases: Discover, Design, and Deliver (Figure I-4). The methodology I share is applicable to all PowerPoint-based learning materials—not just presentations.

Figure I-4. The Three Phases of the PowerPoint Process

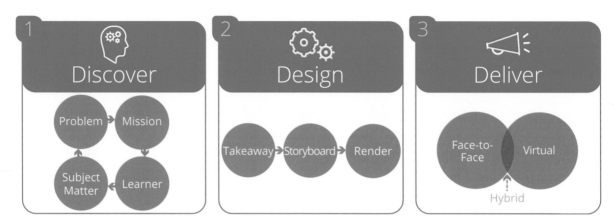

About This Book

Discovery, phase 1, focuses on determining the problem, mission, learner, and subject matter—the four success factors to discovery, and the foundation of an effective presentation (chapter 1). Lacking this information results in a presentation that focuses on you (for example, what you want to say, your biases) and not what your learners need. The outcomes improve the more you know about the problem, mission, learner, and subject matter. Research into what matters most to your audience provides the insight needed to keep them engaged throughout your session and improve adoption rates.

Design, phase 2, is where your presentation is created. This step involves how to write a takeaway (chapter 2), how to storyboard (chapter 3), and the secret tips and tricks to rendering, or making, your slides (chapter 4). Your takeaway is the summary of your entire presentation. It must capture your learners' attention. Storyboarding is your plan. It connects the dots between the takeaway and your narrative. When done right, a proper storyboard is fed by the information found during the discovery phase. All these steps are preparation for understanding the design principles you can then apply to your presentation (chapter 5).

Delivery, phase 3, focuses on your method and medium for sharing your presentation and supporting content. It may be a virtual session; a face-to-face classroom, where participants are learning from a lecture; or both. Best practices, tips, and tricks for each delivery method are included in chapters 6 and 7.

* * *

Being proficient with PowerPoint is only the first step to mastering presentation design and delivery (and any other purpose for which you may use it). The formal steps in this book are intended to give you a solid, repeatable approach to presentation design.

Use what works for your situation. Not every project can accommodate every step in this process. Be judicious when choosing what you need to create a successful presentation with your allocated resources and schedule. For example, you may have four hours to develop a presentation that explains a new technology. In this case, use the steps you have time for.

Finally, although all the steps are important, some matter more than others. The two most important steps in the process are to understand your learner and to develop a takeaway that motivates your audience. These are required to make a successful presentation.

Let's get started. . . .

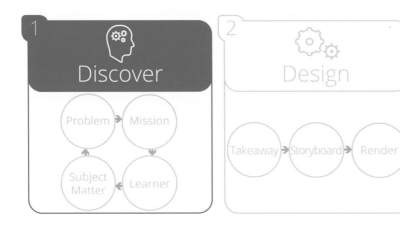

1 Discover

- Problem
- Mission
- Subject Matter
- Learner

2 Design

- Takeaway
- Storyboard
- Render

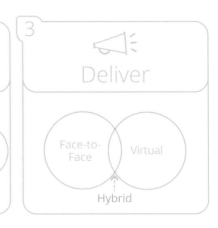

3 Deliver

- Face-to-Face
- Virtual
- Hybrid

Phase 1
Discover

Imagine being tasked to make a presentation for a financial planner. The goal is to empower customers to make wise decisions for their short- and long-term financial security. Right now, with a little research, I suspect you could create a wonderful presentation that shared strategies, formulas, tools, and points of contact you received from your project adviser. You are wise enough to make sure the presentation is professional in every way and takes full advantage of all that PowerPoint has to offer. Assuming you have the information you need, within hours you might have an outline and slides started. If you did this, you would be guilty of what most PowerPoint users fail to do. You would likely make the sort of presentation that you dislike. Engagement and efficacy would suffer.

The main problem with this approach is that you are missing critical pieces of information that directly affect the likelihood your presentation will be successful. For example, what if you discover your audience is people who won the lottery or families with very little money to save and invest? What if you find out that for legal reasons, they cannot invest in traditional retirement saving vehicles? What if your audience is visually impaired? Might any of these significantly change your presentation? (I hope you emphatically answered, "Yes!")

The Discover phase is focused on your audience and its needs—not yours. In this phase, you immerse yourself in the project and see the presentation from multiple perspectives. You become the learner. When done right, you end up with a profile that informs every decision you make during the Design and Deliver phases.

> "When you want to start a PowerPoint presentation, the first thing is: Don't open PowerPoint. You don't want to get lost in the templates, colors, fonts, and design of the slide."
>
> —Doug Thomas, Microsoft, Creates Videos and Training at Support.Microsoft.com

1

The Four Keys to Discovery: Problem, Mission, Learner, and Subject Matter

Most PowerPoint presentations fail because the author does not take time to understand the audience. The author focuses on what they want to say and not what the participants need. Too many assumptions are made about the problem, learners, mission, content, and so on. The developer bases the presentation on their preferences, personality, and biases, and their presentation fails.

Before you develop your presentation, understand the problem you are solving and see it from your learners' perspective. You need to appreciate the requirements and limitations. Your goal is to share solutions to reoccurring problems in a way that achieves their learning objectives.

What is your mission? It should encompass your goals, delivery methods, and resources. Knowing your mission informs what content you include in your presentation and how you communicate and share it. Achieving your audience's learning objectives requires understanding, recollection, and adoption. How you do that in your PowerPoint presentation is dependent upon the learners and the subject matter.

Know your learners. What are their aspirations? What are their hopes, fears, and biases? Do they want to learn this material, or were they told they had to? Your learners' state of mind directly affects their ability to learn. The more you know about them, the greater your odds of engaging them—motivating them to want to learn. They have to decide to care about your content. It is up to you to reinforce or incite that desire.

Lastly, know your subject matter or have access to people who do. How can you teach what you don't know? Your job is to learn and share what is critical to the learning objectives. You have the unenviable task of simplifying complex and sometimes boring content into a desirable, digestible format.

Your goal is to uncover as much intelligence as you can in the time you have, because there will be other things you do not know or cannot control. The more you know, the more you can account for. When it is time to share your PowerPoint presentation and materials, you want to mitigate the risks of anything that will impede learning.

You may also experience less controllable variables that affect whether you reach your learning objectives. I refer to these issues as outside influences; an example is a technical glitch, such as the loss of Internet or power. Do your best to accommodate these variables and roll with them. Your presentation's success is contingent upon the audience's:

- perception (factual or not) of the presenter, material, and environment
- biases
- life experience
- open-mindedness
- intelligence
- subject matter proficiency
- comfort
- state of mind.

Consider the following two scenarios:

1. You create a professionally designed, factually accurate PowerPoint presentation. Unfortunately, the presenter is disheveled and dressed inappropriately, wearing a T-shirt, shorts, and sneakers. The presenter's appearance distracts your audience from the material. Whether your presentation is perceived as credible and factual is now in question.

2. Because of past experience, your audience is biased against the presenter. They may have experienced poor customer service or once owned a defective product made by the presenter's company. Adoption may not occur.

Many juried court systems try to lower the potential risk of outside influences. Lawyers, aware of the damage pre-existing prejudices may have, ask specific questions to eliminate jurors who may result in a loss for their client. In some instances, jurors are sequestered to avoid the likelihood that outside influences will affect their decisions.

Controllable elements (data accuracy, spelling, room temperature) as well as unexpected influences (unintended associations, technical glitches) can determine whether your presentation is given the positive attention required to succeed. For this reason, uncover as many variables as possible during the discovery process. Ensure that everything associated with your presentation is congruent with your mission—your objectives.

After the Discover phase is the Design phase. Design requires planning. At the heart of planning is a combination of research, resources, requirements, and analysis. If you lack certain fundamental information (that is, the problem, mission, learner, and subject matter), your PowerPoint content will be less than effective. For this reason, you want to gather as much relevant data as possible.

The entire Discover phase can be collaborative. For example, one author may have learner insight, another may be a subject matter expert, and still others may hold the remaining pieces of the puzzle. Together, the whole PowerPoint authoring team possesses the necessary knowledge to produce a successful presentation. Your final output is limited only by your (or your group's) imagination and the audience's understanding of the content being shared. Be creative and have fun.

In the Discover phase, you are a detective. Your job is to understand the scope of the project from different perspectives, get into the minds of your learners, learn the subject matter, and use that insight to make the best PowerPoint presentation possible with the time and resources you have.

In my experience, the Discover phase is often ignored. There are two reasons this occurs:

1. **Resources are scarce.** There is a lack of people, money, or time.
2. **There's a lack of understanding.** To make a PowerPoint presentation, the typical first step is to make an outline or get started on the slides. Rarely is discovery the standard approach.

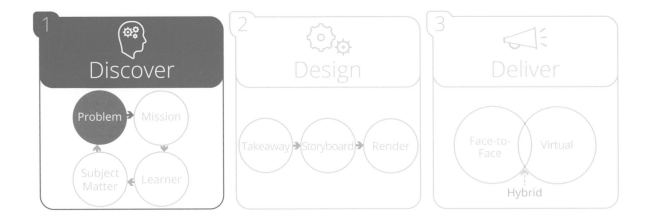

What Is the Problem?

All effective education is inherently solving a problem, and problem solving requires learning. Your presentation should give a solution to an existing problem, or else it has no purpose beyond entertainment or wasting time. The following are four examples of problems that educational PowerPoint presentations solve:

1. A college professor creates a PowerPoint presentation that educates students on Albert Einstein's theory of special relativity. Through this presentation, the professor is solving the students' need to learn this theory to pass the class and advance in the field of physics.

2. A company is implementing new tracking software. The problem is that the existing software does not catalog data and is difficult to search, which affects the organization's ability to respond to client emergencies quickly. They create a training course to help their employees learn and adopt the new software, which is critical to resolving the issue.

3. A not-for-profit organization wants the results of a cancer study. Without an accurate understanding of the findings, additional lives may be lost. A researcher distills the quantitative information and presents it in an easy-to-follow format that allows the organization to quickly analyze the data and create a plan.

4. An organization needs to improve security protocols. The problem is that too many employees fail to observe standard operating procedures and expose the company to unnecessary security risks. They create a mandatory training workshop for their employees to reinforce security processes.

Your audience is sitting through your presentation to improve their condition—to learn something that will help them work through a challenge and achieve a specific goal (or set of goals).

You are not necessarily solving the problem for them, but sharing the solution. You want to impart the knowledge in a way that is succinct, engaging, and illuminating. The audience must want to apply what they learn, or else the problem will remain.

For inspiration, check out TED Talks (www.ted.com), in which experts across industries share solutions with the world. The most popular TED Talks help people solve a problem—either in their work or personal lives. Here are some of my favorites:

- Ken Robinson's "Do Schools Kill Creativity?" discusses improving learning for children.
- Simon Sinek's "How Great Leaders Inspire Action" tells you how to motivate others.
- Jill Bolte Taylor's "My Stroke of Insight" helps learners understand what happens in our brain when you or someone you know has a stroke.

PowerPoint is absent in each of these presentations, yet they are extremely popular. Why? In part, they solve a problem. Education solves problems.

Successful PowerPoint training presentations solve the learner's problem. However, you must first understand the problem before you can create a presentation that provides a solution.

Formalize the problem by completing a Solution Matrix (Table 1-1), which helps you explore the problem ("As Is" column), goals ("To Be" column), and barriers. (The "To Be" column is addressed in greater detail in the next section.)

Table 1-1. The Parts of a Solution Matrix

As Is	To Be	Barrier(s)
What is the problem now? How does it work now?	What is the ideal (and realistic) goal state?	What is stopping the change?

Start by listing the current situation in the "As Is" column. What are the problems the learner faces today? How does it work now? Perhaps the issue is they fail to follow a procedure, they lack knowledge needed to complete a task, or the current tool they use takes too long to process data. Figure out the problem and capture it.

Next, write down the "To Be" state. Be realistic and summarize at a high level; detail isn't important now. At this point, you are focusing on the problem and the barriers.

Finally, list the barriers that prevent the goal from happening. If these obstacles were removed, the problem would be resolved. The "As Is" state would become the "To Be." The barriers are the foundation upon which you will build your solution during storyboarding. The presented solution should remove your learners' barriers.

The Solution Matrix gets you closer to the situation. When properly filled out, it will give you a better appreciation of what learners experience. Your goal is to empathize as much as possible with learners. Seeing through your audience's eyes will improve your PowerPoint content's effectiveness.

Table 1-2 is an example of a Solution Matrix with the As Is and Barrier columns completed.

Table 1-2. Creating a Solution Matrix

As Is	To Be	Barrier(s)
Files are shared openly over email and removable storage devices, which is a security risk.		• The secure network is seen as more time consuming. • Using the secure network is not as intuitive. • Using the secure network is not a habit.

In most instances, there is a prescribed solution. For example, you are tasked with creating a PowerPoint presentation that educates learners on a new tool meant to solve their existing problems. Part of the Discovery process has been completed for you. When this is the case, explore the problem even more. Improve your understanding and, at your discretion, validate that the proposed solution solves your audience's problem. If it does, ensure this connection is clear to the learners. We will learn more about how to do this in the Design phase.

Be specific when uncovering the learners' problem. A difficult-to-explain problem is almost impossible to resolve, whereas a well-defined problem has a well-defined solution. Verify that your audience knows the issue you are solving. Most times, your target audience is aware of the challenge you are working out, but it doesn't hurt to remind them.

Once you discover the problem and barriers, define the goals, understand your audience, and learn the subject matter well enough to present the solution in a way that's easy to remember and apply.

I used my Solution Matrix when I was helping a large hotel chain develop a presentation for hotel owners. After chatting with my point of contact (my subject matter expert), it was clear to both of us that the problem was lost revenue and low occupancy rates. We easily determined the goal state to be increased revenue and higher occupancy rates. The barriers took a little more investigation, but once we uncovered all of them, we were able to develop a powerful presentation that, if followed, would absolutely achieve their goals.

The presenter could clearly and simply articulate the problem, which resonated with participants, as well as the benefits of doing what he was sharing (the "To Be"). Next, he shared the three ways hotel operators could eliminate the barriers to achieve those goals. That's the power of using this approach. Participants relate to your content, and it empowers them to achieve whatever you decide is the best outcome.

Here is a best-practice checklist for understanding the problem:

☐ **Know the problem you're solving.**

☐ **List barriers that prevent the problem from being solved.**

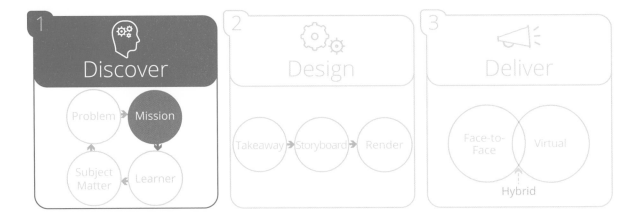

What Is Your Mission?

Define your mission, which is the optimal outcomes using specific delivery methods and resources. Your mission clarifies the critical conditions and benchmarks that your presentation must achieve to succeed. It consists of four variables: goals, measures, requirements, and resources.

Goals

Your goals are your learning objectives. Andy Bounds, author of *The Jelly Effect* (2007), says it's all about the "afters." What do your learners get after the presentation, after they review your PowerPoint learning materials, after they applied what they learned? If your audience will receive no benefit and fail to resolve a problem, why should they care? If participants don't care, why will they pay attention? Know their "afters." They should be synonymous with your goals.

Choosing goals can be challenging. There are three groups that have their own goals, and they don't always align:

1. your participants
2. your client (the person who engaged your services)
3. your organization.

Sometimes these groups complement one another, and other times they contradict. When possible, find a way to synthesize everyone's goals. For your presentation to be effective, you must weigh each to determine how best to proceed. When in doubt, focus on your learners' goals.

Consolidate and simplify when possible. Fewer goals result in a more effective PowerPoint presentation. Your job is to remove complexity and streamline every aspect of your training content, which includes all tasks during the Discover phase.

The goal state must be realistic and achievable. For example, if the problem is poor health due to an unhealthy lifestyle, the audience's end goal is unlikely to be having the body of an Olympic athlete. If it is unrealistic, do not list it as a goal. Decide what the future state is and write it down.

Be specific. Make sure your goals are observable or measurable. You cannot improve the effectiveness of your PowerPoint materials if you have no way of assessing success.

Use action verbs like *complete, identify,* and *deliver* when setting your goals. Keep it simple, clear, and to the point. The more verbose or convoluted the goals, the less likely they will be achieved. Here are three examples of well-constructed learning goals:

1. Participants can increase revenue and occupancy rates by applying three solutions.
2. Attendees can resolve IT issues by identifying the source of an issue within 10 minutes.
3. Learners are able to complete a dietary analysis for a one-month nutritional plan.
4. By the end of this presentation, students can identify the artist, year, and art movement of all artwork shared.

Add the goals to your Solution Matrix. Each one should align with the problem and barriers. If all barriers were removed and the problem solved, what would the outcome be?

Table 1-3 is an example of a completed Solution Matrix. It shows how the problem, barriers, and goals are related.

Table 1-3. Example of a Completed Solution Matrix

As Is	To Be	Barrier(s)
Files are shared openly over email and removable storage devices, which is a security risk.	Files are only shared using the secure network.	• The secure network is seen as more time consuming. • Using the secure network is not as intuitive. • Using the secure network is not a habit.

Measures

How do you know if you have reached your goals? You need to validate. A mature learning system includes benchmarks—a way to measure success. There are two paths from which to choose:

1. **Direct Measures:** Evaluate and validate through direct evidence of education. A few examples of direct measures include:
   » the work created during the class
   » the observable work products delivered after the class
   » testing scores.

2. **Indirect Measures:** Evaluate learner perceptions of the education to validate if your content met expectations. A few examples of indirect measures include surveys, interviews, and questionnaires.

> Complementary to my approach are SMART goals. The acronym is meant to help you pick goals that are specific, measurable, agreed to, realistic, and time based. Learn more by searching for "SMART goals" online or reading a book like *S.M.A.R.T. Goals Made Simple* by S.J. Scott (2014).

Focus on the learning that occurs as a result of your program when you determine how to measure its success. The type of process or tool doesn't matter as long as an assessment occurs. Determining success requires assessment.

Direct and indirect measures are often used together to give an overall review of the results. The more you track the results, the faster your PowerPoint skills improve because you are able to correlate key success factors with your approach.

Whatever you choose, make it an integral part of your learning event. Embrace validation and use it to grow. Measure and adjust accordingly for continual improvement.

Requirements

Following the project requirements paves the way to a successful training session. What is the delivery method? What is acceptable to share? What can't you share?

Table 1-4 contains examples of requirements you should identify as early as possible. To improve the odds that I define all conditions and obligations, I split the information into two categories: technical and procedural.

Table 1-4. Creating a List of Technical and Procedural Requirements

Technical	Procedural
Which version of PowerPoint can you use?	What is the duration or time limit?
Is it projected? If yes, what are the specifications of the projector/display device? What is the size of the projected surface and the room? How much seating is there?	Are there specified break times?
Can you use your laptop, or must you use another computer?	Is there a sign-in sheet?
Is it presented on a Mac or Windows operating system?	Will your PowerPoint content be printed, online with a trainer, online self-led, face-to-face with a trainer, or a hybrid?

Technical	Procedural
Are animations acceptable?	Will you need exercises, worksheets/books, or breakout sessions?
Is video OK?	Do you need a timer?
Are you using specialty fonts for branding? (Can fonts be embedded?)	Must you follow a brand standard or use an existing PowerPoint template?
Are there software security tools?	Are you working with others?
Is there audio?	Are there security protocols?
Can you use a camera?	Is lunch provided?
What is the lighting in the room?	What learning materials are you expected to furnish?

When you get a requirement that limits your ability to deliver the best possible solution, ask your client or point of contact why. When you learn the answer, you may be able to reassure them that their needs will be met without this requirement.

For instance, I once developed a PowerPoint presentation that shared a new product with potential partners. My client wanted almost everything to be animated, so I asked why. He said he wanted the presentation to communicate that his solution was cutting edge. He believed animations would convey innovation. Once I understood his reason for the request, I was able to work with him to deliver a PowerPoint presentation that met his goals and effectively educated his future partners without unnecessary animation.

"Filling out an intake form is the best way to discover what a client presentation needs to be. A good intake form asks for info like the speaker's objective, room setting, audience size, print requirements . . . many points of data."

—Tony Ramos,
The Presentationist

Another example: When I created PowerPoint templates for BMW Financial Services, they wanted all their graphics created in PowerPoint and not in other software like Adobe Illustrator. When I asked why, they replied that they wanted to easily modify graphics as needed without having to call me (or an in-house designer) to make changes. I realized that as long as the graphics were editable in PowerPoint, I could include elements that did not originate from within the tool. I delivered a better product faster by using a combination of PowerPoint's native elements and items brought in from other sources that were completely editable in PowerPoint.

Seek first to understand a requirement before debating or dismissing it. Uncover the reason for the demand if you think it will hinder the likelihood of success. When a client insists on an unexpected requirement, consider responding with, "That sounds great. We can absolutely do it. Out of curiosity, why do you say that?" Once you know why, you might know a better way to do it and find a better solution for the client—a win-win for you both!

When I am my own client and I make my own requirements, I sometimes ask myself the same question, "Why?" Why do I feel compelled to do this? If my answer does not help achieve the defined goals, I remove the requirement.

Resources

What roles, processes, tools, and knowledge do you have and need? To develop your PowerPoint presentation, you want to take stock of what you possess and what you must acquire.

What roles need to be filled and who can fill them? Usually, subject matter experts are paramount. Depending on the project's scope, you may need designers, writers, and editors. Often, you are all of the above—in which case, discipline yourself to follow a proven process for defining resources to ensure you have what is needed.

Processes ensure repeatable success of your training. Do you have existing processes in place to speed development? Do you need a version control procedure for your slides? List the processes you need now and in the future. Perhaps you will need a way to share large files or keep PowerPoint slides from being edited by contributors. Recognize it now before it slows your progress later. If a new procedure is needed, identify it and develop it for your next project.

Tools speed development, so decide what tools are needed. For example, do you need the ability to poll your audience? Do you have access to a tool that can be embedded into PowerPoint? Catalog what tools you will use with PowerPoint to execute your project.

There are often gaps in the knowledge you have and the knowledge needed to complete a project. What specific information is required? Once you identify the information or expertise needed, it makes it easier to track down an expert or identify a website, book, or resource that helps you bridge that gap.

To track the information, consider a matrix approach to quickly assess what you have and what you need (Figure 1-1).

Tip: When hiring others, be sure they are professionally trained and experienced in the software and type of work required to complete the task. Review their resumes, portfolios, and past performances.

Figure 1-1. A Matrix Approach to Assessment

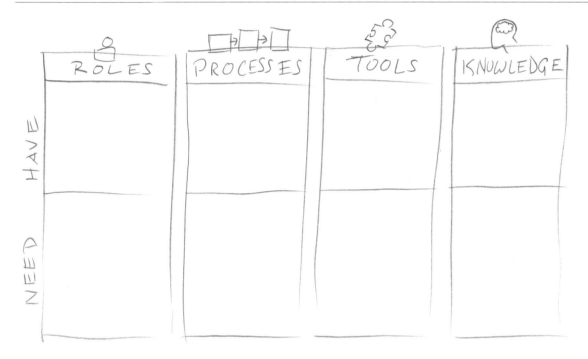

Knowing your goals, requirements, and resources early in the process eliminates hiccups, headaches, and wasted time. Waiting until the need arises slows the process and could derail the project. Use this best-practice checklist to remind you of your key mission factors:

- ☐ **List the goals.**
- ☐ **Include a way to measure success directly and indirectly.**
- ☐ **Define requirements (technical and procedural).**
- ☐ **Define resources you have and need for roles, processes, tools, and knowledge.**

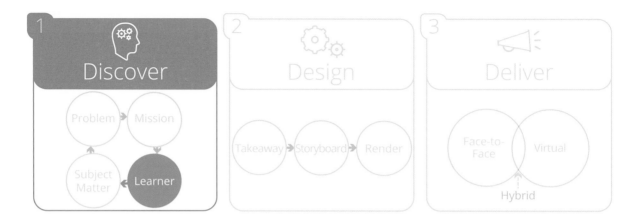

Who Is Your Learner?

Most PowerPoint presentations fail because the author concentrates on the subject matter and what they want to say instead of the learners. Your audience is focused on what they want from you. What do they get as a result of your presentation? If they cannot see themselves reflected in your content, their attention wanes and adoption rates fall.

Most presentations emphasize the subject matter and not the learners because it's easy to explain the topic and difficult to connect it to your audience's goals. Your content must relate to your learners' hopes. To do so requires a level of intimacy that many presenters fail to appreciate.

Know your learners. Who are they—academics who love learning? Employees forced to take your safety training? What language do they speak? What are their buzzwords? What are their hot buttons? What motivates them? What do they like or dislike—colors, imagery, detailed explanations?

If you don't know much about your audience, find out! Ask them questions. Research their organization. Visit their website. Talk with those who know them better than you, such as current or former employees or their clients. The more you know, the more powerful your presentation. Your goal is to feel what your audience feels. Empathize with your audience so your content captivates their attention and they can easily comprehend it. Every student will be different; it's your job to find the common denominators. Look for things that help or hinder training. There are three key areas for learner understanding: proficiency, concerns, and preferred learning approach.

Tip: It is subconsciously comforting to hear and see familiar things. When applicable, use words, images, and sounds that your audience knows to build trust.

Proficiency

Have you heard someone use an acronym you did not know? Were you ever lost while learning something new? Have you attended a PowerPoint presentation that was not advanced enough for you? How did it make you feel? Frustration sets in when we struggle with confusing information or become disinterested due to irrelevant content. It results in a host of negative feelings.

If your audience finds your PowerPoint content to be beyond or behind their skill level, they will tune out. Determining your audience's proficiency helps you choose a communication style and an approach to explain your content. How well do your learners know the subject matter? At what level are they? Are they new to the material, skilled at it, or subject matter experts? For example, if your participants are beginners and the topic is complex, use a metaphor to help them relate to and understand your topic. If your audience is advanced, avoid reiterating what they already know. Use the appropriate technical terms, acronyms, and imagery they're familiar with. Explanations should build off their existing expertise.

[
"I make it a rule to believe only what I understand."
—Benjamin Disraeli
]

Proficiency can be determined through formal assessments (tests), performance reviews, and conversations with your target audience or those close to them, such as management or co-workers.

Concerns

What are the key concerns that will affect your audience's ability to learn the material? Specifically, what are their likes, dislikes, and biases—as it relates to your PowerPoint material. Knowing your learners' preferences helps you connect your content with those things that are favored. Understanding audience dislikes and biases uncovers obstacles that block an open mind and hinder learning. I define a bias as a pre-existing prejudice for or against some aspect of what you are teaching. It could be a company, tool, process, person, color, word, solution, sound, and so on.

I was once hired to conduct a PowerPoint workshop in Minneapolis. I used a bridge metaphor in one of my explanations and it was met with pushback. Unknown to me, in 2007, the I-35W Mississippi River eight-lane bridge collapsed, killing 13 people and injuring 145 more. Obviously, had I known about the tragedy, I would have used a different metaphor. My ignorance brought negative emotions into a discussion instead of positive, open thoughts. Do your homework. Uncover as many biases as possible. By understanding your audience's likes, dislikes, and biases, you are more likely to keep them focused on the topic and not distracted by unwanted tangents.

Preferred Learning Approach

Does your audience prefer individual or group exercises? If so, what type? Do they like to discuss topics or would they rather watch a video clip? Because learner preferences vary, I use a variety of approaches in my presentations that are relevant to the content and objectives. Interactivity is almost always a great option. Here are six ways to learn more about your target audience:

1. **Ask and listen.** Have a conversation with your participants. Ask questions and take notes. To dig deeper into their psyche, I will ask this question after a learner has shared a response with the class: "That's a great point. Why do you say that?" Encourage your learner to share more. Guide them. Get insight into their proficiency, concerns, and preferred learning approach. By asking, not only do you get accurate insight, but you also make your participants believe they matter. Your audience has input into what they will learn, which makes them more invested.

2. **Observe.** Watch how your learners do their jobs and socialize. What is easy and what is challenging? What makes them smile and what frustrates them? Their body language gives vital intelligence to their true feelings.

3. **Review their records.** Examine test scores, reviews, accolades, and issues. Look for patterns and make logical inferences. For example, a group of participants may receive awards for always shipping products early. This indicates they are process and task driven. If you give them a task, they will concentrate on accomplishing that activity.

4. **Distribute surveys and questionnaires.** Ask your learners specific questions that help you determine their proficiency, concerns, and preferred learning approach. For example, ask them to rate a set of predefined goals from one to three, with one being critical and three being least important to achieve.

5. **Create extracurricular activities.** Set up "getting to know you" events. Icebreakers, games, and sports work well, as long as there is a definitive purpose for each activity that maps back to a benefit to your learners.

6. **Use LEM.** When I struggle to understand my learners, I use the Learner Empathy Map (LEM) exercise (Figure 1-2). You can construct your LEM on a whiteboard or piece of paper, or with mind-mapping software. Write likes, dislikes, and biases in the center. Next, radiating out from the middle, list those elements that align with each central category. Continue to branch out as you further define and explain each element. Use this insight to craft the right content, messages, and story.

Once, when developing a proposal for a government contractor, my team could not agree on our target audience's likes, dislikes, and biases, so we made an LEM (Figure 1-3). First, to improve empathy, we chose a set of representative learners we personally knew. If you do not know your learners, give them names.

Figure 1-2. Learner Empathy Map

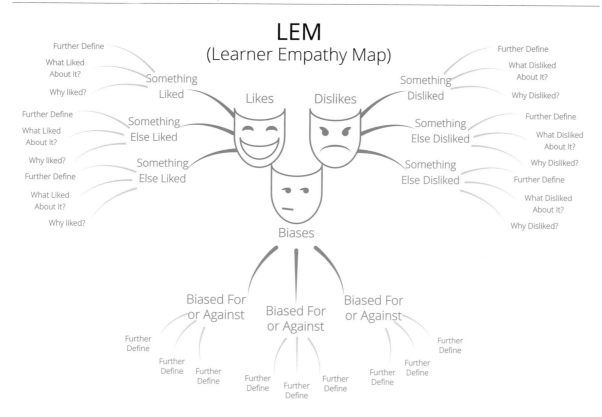

Make your learners as real as possible—fictitious or not. On a piece of paper, we listed the three central categories—likes, dislikes, and biases. What we listed was based on personal interactions, online research, and educated guesses. Once complete, I used that information to pick a path forward. I made a PowerPoint infographic that was easy to use, included examples, was relevant to their current project, and ensured consistency among writers and reviewers. It was a great success.

In chapter 2, you will learn about the Learner Motivation Map (LMM) and how to formally define learner motivations. The LEM emphasizes the audience partialities and potential landmines to avoid, whereas the LMM focuses on learner motivations. Neither is necessary to complete if you have an intimate understanding of your learners. The LEM and LMM help you better understand your target audience, enabling you to tailor your PowerPoint content to them, which significantly increases the likelihood of success.

Figure 1-3. Hand-Drawn Learner Empathy Map

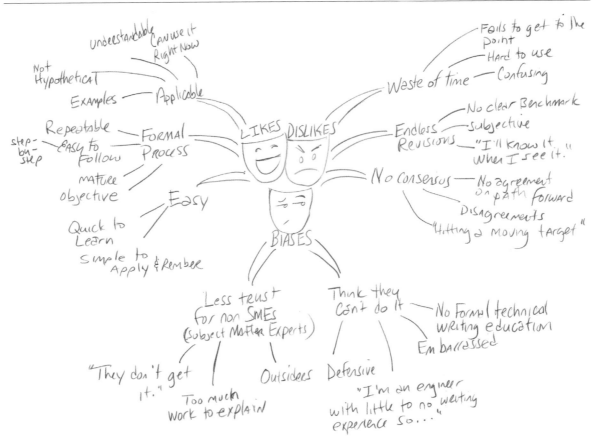

Here is a best-practice checklist for understanding your learners:

☐ Focus on your learners (not yourself).

☐ Uncover your learners':

    ☐ proficiency with the subject matter

    ☐ concerns (likes, dislikes, and biases)

    ☐ preferred learning style.

☐ Use the six investigative strategies as needed.

☐ Use your findings to pick a path forward and inform future decisions.

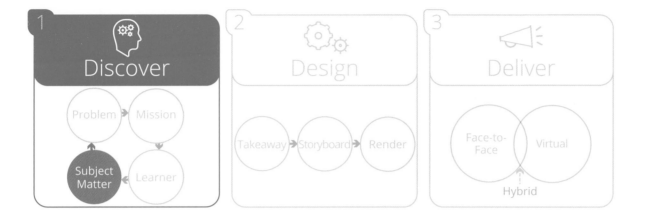

What Is Your Subject Matter?

Know your subject matter. You must know the topic to teach it. It is your job to align the subject matter with the problem, mission, and learner in a clear, compelling way. The more you know, the more likely your audience will understand.

Here are five efficient ways to learn more about your subject matter. Use one or more to quickly study the topic at hand (WikiHow 2016):

1. Ask a subject matter expert.
2. Research.
3. Observe.
4. Gain hands-on experience.
5. Attend classes.

Subject Matter Expert

Learn from the wisdom of others. Ask specific questions to get specific answers. And take notes: In my experience, people ask good questions, but fail to take good notes. I once supported a project in which a SME shared her engineering expertise. The authors listened closely with their arms crossed. One day later, the authors were asking the SME questions that had been answered the day before. Write it down so you can remember what was shared. It shows that you value the SME's time and expertise.

Research

Go to your favorite search engine and enter the topic. If one search fails to deliver the desired results, change your search terms. Look for visuals and infographics that explain your topic; don't limit

Tip: If you don't know something, don't lie. Always tell the truth. Our learners' brains are incredible lie detectors. For example, a neuroscientist had participants play card games with decks of rigged cards set to produce unfair results. Skin-conductance tests revealed that the participants became nervous when reaching for the rigged cards long before the suspicion that they were using rigged cards reached their conscious minds (Renvoisé and Morin 2005).

yourself to websites. Visit the library. Read books, articles, and whitepapers. Watch videos.

Make sure your sources are reputable. Check credentials, references, popularity, comments, and reviews. When in doubt, research the authors of the learning materials to make sure they are reputable.

Observation

Observe those who are proficient in what you are teaching. Shadow them as they perform the task. Watch and learn. Take notes. When needed and possible, ask clarifying questions. Imagine you have to do what they did. Could you? If you think you could, you are on the right track.

To make an interactive surgical game, I was once tasked with creating a tutorial for open heart surgery for a medical IT company. After I watched videos and read as much as I could, my boss, a doctor himself, made special arrangements for me to sit in on the actual surgery. Nervous and steps away from the patient, I watched as the cardiac surgeon performed the entire procedure—from incision to sutures. I took notes and pictures, and made sure to stay out of the way. Power cords, machines, and medical personnel were everywhere, so capturing the information I needed wasn't easy—but it was incredibly valuable. I left the surgery with a deeper understanding of what happens during this operation, and my firsthand experience resulted in a better presentation. To this day, there is a tiny part of me that thinks, "If I absolutely had to, I could do that!" And at the same time, I know I could never do it. That is the power of intent observation.

Hands-On Experience

Do it! Although a do-it-yourself approach is not the most efficient means to learn, trial and error is an effective teacher. Get your hands dirty and embrace failing forward. Each time you are unsuccessful, you discover a way that doesn't work and get one step closer to uncovering what does.

Due to accessibility, expertise needed, and other factors, hands-on experience isn't usually a viable option. When it is, use your judgment to decide if it is the best use of your time.

Of course, most times you cannot get so hands-on. For example, using the previous observation example, I am certain that if I learned and performed open heart surgery, the training materials would be better than they were. I knew that would never (ever, ever) happen, so I observed instead.

Classes

Enroll in a workshop, search YouTube for educational videos, or attend an online course. The following is a list of some of the highest-rated online resources:

- CreativeLive (www.creativelive.com)
- Coursera (www.coursera.org)
- Coursmos (www.coursmos.com)
- Curious (http://curious.com)
- edX (www.edx.org)
- Highbrow (www.gohighbrow.com)
- Lynda.com (www.lynda.com)
- Skillshare (www.skillshare.com)
- Udemy (www.udemy.com).

For instance, I learned how to render professional isometric graphics for use in PowerPoint from one of the best designers in the world through an online class. His expertise was downloaded and assimilated for a fraction of the cost and time it would have taken me to learn through trial and error.

Here is a best-practice checklist for understanding the subject matter:

☐ **Know your subject matter.**
☐ **Pick one or more ways to do so:**
　☐ **Ask a subject matter expert.**
　☐ **Research.**
　☐ **Observe.**
　☐ **Get hands-on experience.**
　☐ **Take a class.**

Summary

That completes the Discover phase. Knowing the problem and mission, and understanding the learner and subject matter, are critical when developing a powerful PowerPoint presentation. However, most of my projects are quick-turn, and I don't have the time to do every step I shared. Be flexible and realistic. Pick and choose what you need most.

On my projects, I always know all four Discover factors (problem, mission, learner, and subject matter) but, sometimes, it is only a high-level view of each. Gather as much information as you can with the time you have, because the more you know, the better your presentation.

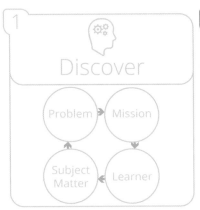

1 Discover

Problem → Mission
↑ ↓
Subject Matter ← Learner

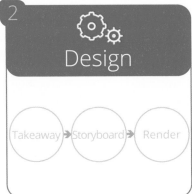

2 Design

Takeaway → Storyboard → Render

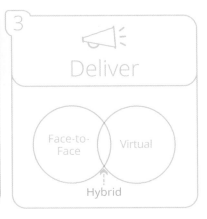

3 Deliver

Face-to-Face | Virtual
Hybrid

Phase 2 Design

In this phase of the PowerPoint development life cycle, you plan and make your Power-Point slides and support materials. The Design phase focuses on three key steps:

1. **Write your takeaway.** Your takeaway is a simple message that summarizes your entire presentation and motivates your audience to want to learn. It is the keystone of your training materials: slides, workbook, handouts, and so on. Start with a significant, provocative message and build your story around it.

2. **Storyboard your presentation and learning materials.** Storyboarding is your plan. It is the fastest way to block out your presentation, slides, infographics, and any other learning materials you plan to make with PowerPoint. Storyboarding saves time and money, and ensures your presentation tells a story and supports your takeaway.

3. **Render your content using PowerPoint.** Proper construction, architecture, layout, and style are the foundations for success. Professional slide design quickly communicates to your learners that you, your presentation, and your support materials are organized, ordered, and worth their attention.

What I share in this book isn't about only making the best PowerPoint product or producing slides fast. It's both. Time and money are often scarce commodities when developing PowerPoint content. You are frequently asked to do a lot in little time with limited resources. Following the three key steps in the Design phase ensures that you will efficiently deliver the best product. Unlike the Discover phase, the Design phase should be followed as I have laid it out (with a few exceptions that you identify based on your unique situation). When I have failed to follow this process, I have been forced to do several revisions, which cost time and money.

2

Writing a Powerful Takeaway

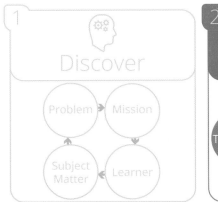

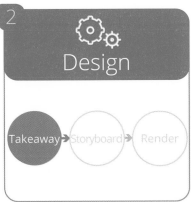

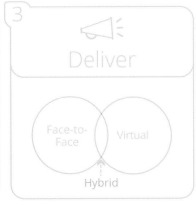

A takeaway inspires and motivates your audience to want to learn what is being presented. It is the point of your content. Think of it as a newspaper headline; if it doesn't grab attention, people are less likely to read the article. Similarly, if the learners are not invested and engaged from the beginning, your presentation will fail to be effective.

Training requires engagement. Our goal as instructors and talent developers is to improve understanding, recollection, and adoption. To achieve each of these, learners must want to learn the content. Our job is to support or ignite their desire by giving them a reason to care and shepherd them through the learning life cycle. Their reward for being a part of our presentation should be obvious; we must connect our messages, narrative, and slides to what they will receive after they use what we shared. That benefit—increased sales, effective communications, higher staff confidence—is the first part of your takeaway.

Understanding What Motivates Your Learners

Participants ask me, "How do I motivate someone through a PowerPoint presentation?" The answer is simple once you know how the human brain makes a decision to learn or not.

Everyone is motivated by three things: pain, fear, and gain. Decisions are predicated on these factors. They are the reasons we are inspired to learn new things and change. Without at least one of these influencers, learners have no reason to alter their behavior (Figure 2-1).

Figure 2-1. Motivating Learning

Pain, fear, and gain are interrelated. Let's say a learner must adopt a new tool:

- **Pain:** The current tool is slow and frustrating.
- **Fear:** The inefficiency of the current tool may negatively affect the perception of their competence and adversely affect their compensation and career.
- **Gain:** The new tool is faster and easier, and helps learners do a better job, which may positively affect performance and improve their compensation.

Although these motivators work together, each elicits a different emotional response from your audience, so you don't want to base your presentation narrative on all three. This helps keep your takeaway simple. If you split your key message between the three, you risk confusing your audience. You could discuss the other motivators within your presentation as long as they are not the focus—the primary takeaway. Consider how learners might react to each motivator and choose the best option for your goals.

> "Want change to happen?
> Create a sense of urgency."
>
> —Sam Horn, TEDx Speaker,
> Intrigue Agency

For instance, in my PowerPoint courses, I ask participants what they want to gain from the workshop. I write down their goals and assure each person that they will achieve them. I then tie everything to a higher-level benefit so that it all links to one succinct, clear message. For example, I might say, "You will get one giant step closer to being a PowerPoint ninja." To be a PowerPoint ninja, participants must reach the goals we listed. In my experience, a simple message, or takeaway, improves understanding, recollection, and adoption.

Pain reminds your audience of their current discomfort. It gives your learners an emotional reason to adopt a new tool because they are prompted to recall how poorly the existing tool makes them feel. People are strongly motivated to stop painful situations and move toward pleasurable conditions.

Fear of loss prepares your audience to react to a dangerous situation. It is more persuasive than gain (Kahneman and Tversky 1984). Use fear for difficult-to-motivate learners. For example, learners mandated to adopt a new tool may need a fear-focused takeaway to improve adoption rates.

Gain promises your audience a benefit or set of benefits. I recommend focusing on gain in your takeaway. Positive outcomes—compared with the negative characteristics of pain and fear—create an encouraging, optimistic story for your presentation. Gain is more likely to put your learner in a receptive frame of mind. For this reason, your takeaway should include explicit or implicit benefits (gain). I always start with gain. If I discover that some participants are not invested in learning, I weave in pain and fear later.

Focusing on fear (and pain) in your takeaway elicits negative emotions that may affect your audience's ability to process and absorb your content. A presentation highlighting negative aspects and not the positive outcomes may impede learning, because your audience is likely to recall the outcomes that can hurt them and not much else. To improve survival rates,

Tip: According to Alan Deutschman in his 2007 book *Change or Die*, for fear to work as a motivator, there must be hope that the negative outcome can be avoided. For this reason, your presentation should offer that hope.

humans are programmed to give more weight to things that can hurt us. Your audience may fixate on pain or fear and become distracted from learning the new material.

Empathy is the secret to developing motivators that resonate with your audience. As mentioned earlier, your goal is to better understand your target audience and uncover their motivations to mitigate the likelihood that your takeaway will hinder learning. See it from your audience's perspective—not yours, not your company's, and not your client's. What are their hopes and fears? What do they dream about? What keeps them up at night? Focus on the positive outcomes that occur after they have successfully applied their newly acquired knowledge and skills.

> "Action springs out of what we fundamentally desire."
>
> —Harry A. Overstreet,
> *Influencing Human Behavior* (2003)

You must include an explicit or implicit motivator if you want engagement. Your learners should be able to identify the benefits to them. It doesn't matter how they know it. Occasionally the motivator is intuitive, or it's written in the slide title. Sometimes it may be shared through a story, exercise, or game. When learners are aware of the benefits, they will connect with the material.

Use the Learner Motivation Map (LMM) to formally define learner motivations. This approach helps uncover previously unknown insights. To populate the LMM, list the pains, gains, and fears of your target audience. It can be one or many for each of the three motivators (Figure 2-2).

Figure 2-2. Learner Motivation Map

What pain does the audience experience as a result of **not** learning?

What does the audience gain as a result of learning?

What does the audience fear will happen as a result of **not** learning?

Another technique is to use the phrase *so that* . . . to uncover high-level benefits (gains) that resonate with your audience. The following example is written from the learners' perspective: "I'm learning a new tool *so that* my job can get done faster *so that* I don't have to stay late every night *so that* I can spend more time doing the things I love to do."

Structuring Your Takeaway

Insight into your audience's hopes and fears, coupled with what you learned during the Discover phase, ensures that you pick the motivators you believe will keep them engaged. The more you understand your learners and practice writing motivation-driven takeaways, the easier it becomes.

I recommend the following structure when writing takeaway statements to ensure your message is clear and concise. It quickly shares what matters most to the learners and how to get it (Figure 2-3).

Figure 2-3. Structure for Takeaway Statements

The first part of your takeaway statement (Motivator) gives your learner a reason to care, and the second part (By What Means) tells them how they will achieve the promised goal. It clearly and succinctly informs your audience what they will gain and what actions are required to receive what is promised.

While the takeaway is usually one sentence, you can separate it into two short sentences. The first sentence is the motivator; the second sentence shares the means by which the motivator is achieved.

The following takeaways use pain, gain, or fear to incentivize an audience to adopt new practices shared in a presentation. The target audience consists of people in their 60s learning new fitness habits.

PAIN	GAIN	FEAR
Stop feeling bad by doing two things every week.	Feel better by doing two things every week.	Prevent the crippling pain that can come with aging. Do these two things every week.

Each takeaway elicits different emotions. Pain and fear rely on undesirable concepts and discontent, whereas gain uses constructive encouragement. Fear is most likely to receive initial audience engagement, but may feel heavy-handed and manipulative, which affects learner trust. Research proves that negative words used in pain- and fear-focused takeaways, such as *stop* or *don't*, are less likely to result in acceptance and change. Negative and positive words stimulate different areas of our brains (Newberg and Waldman 2012). Starting with encouragement increases the odds that your learners remain open and receptive to your presentation.

Always write your takeaway before developing your slides. Allow your takeaway to drive content development. Most PowerPoint instructors write their takeaway as an afterthought. They use it as a hindsight summary of the completed presentation, slide, or support document. The correct approach is to begin with the message. Connect the learning objectives to the resulting benefits before you develop slides. Knowing your takeaway first improves the outcome and lowers your level of effort when building new presentations.

"Before you begin assembling your presentation, write a bumper sticker for it—a few words that control and encapsulate your entire message. Put this bumper sticker on a sticky note at the top of your computer and then pressure test every slide and bit of information you are thinking of including. If it doesn't support the bumper sticker in some way, it is extraneous and should be cut."

—Nolan Haims,
Microsoft PowerPoint MVP

Your learners must know your takeaway as soon as possible. Even if it's not written or said, your audience must understand the WIIFM (What's in it for me?). If your audience sees no benefit, their attention drifts. Give your learners a reason to care about what happens next.

Whenever possible, confirm that your takeaway engages your audience by asking them in person, over email, or through any other form of communication. If you cannot communicate directly with your learners, ask someone who is close with them. Your takeaway is the point of your entire presentation. If it's wrong, you will fail.

When starting a new PowerPoint assignment, I interview at least one audience member once I know my mission. Be sure to choose participants who reflect most of your audience's desires. For example, if I have 19 HR managers and one engineer attending my workshop, and I had to choose only one participant to chat with, I'd spend time with an HR manager. My objective is to uncover, repeat back, and verify the primary takeaway that resonates with my learners. I ask, "Would you want to attend a session that showed you how to lower your workload using the five improvements we discussed?" If the learner answers yes, I can now write my primary takeaway: "Lower your workload through five easy changes."

Making sure your audience knows your takeaway early contextualizes all that you share. The learners are grounded and can easily connect the dots back to the big picture. Figure 2-4 shows the right and wrong ways to develop and introduce your primary takeaway.

Figure 2-4. Right and Wrong Ways to Develop the Takeaway

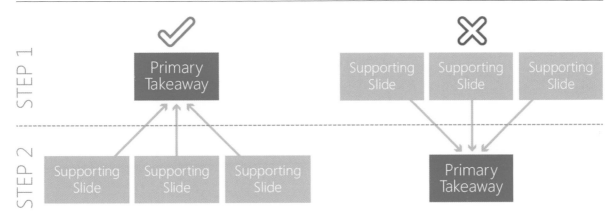

Include no more than three benefits (gain motivators) in one takeaway, such as, "Save money and time and make your job easier using our new app." The more benefits you add in one takeaway, the more each is diluted, which weakens its impact. If you uncover more than three key motivators, consolidate many into one and share the supporting influencers in subsequent slides. For example, after your presentation, your learners will receive:

- **Benefit 1:** Process more orders with automation.
- **Benefit 2:** Respond faster to trouble tickets.
- **Benefit 3:** Decrease the number of trouble tickets.
- **Benefit 4:** Spend less time with paperwork.

In this case, we can either delete a less influential benefit or summarize the four benefits into an overarching, high-level benefit: "Make your job easier." The resulting primary takeaway may read, "Make your job easier by using the new help desk software." The other benefits become supporting slides (supporting takeaways) that validate or explain how the learners' jobs become easier. Figure 2-5 illustrates the supportive slides that reinforce and explain how the new help desk software makes the learners' jobs easier using the four original benefits.

Figure 2-5. Benefits Become Supporting Slides

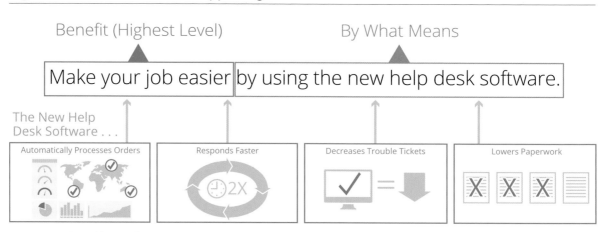

As Benjamin Franklin once said, "I have already made this paper too long, for which I must crave pardon, not having now time to make it shorter." It is not easy to summarize your presentation into a one-sentence primary takeaway; however, the rewards for this up-front work are exponentially beneficial. Creating a motivational takeaway before developing slides:

- saves time and lowers cost by minimizing the level of effort to develop your presentation
- lowers the number of slides made and reworked, because only content germane to your message matters
- improves your success rate because learner engagement increases; improved engagement fuels adoption rates.

Figure 2-6 demonstrates how to use a benefit-driven takeaway to drive the development of your presentation. In this example, the company wants to save money. If management adopts a new approach, this objective can be achieved. The managers' compensation is directly tied to cost reduction. The benefit could have been "increase your compensation," but I chose "reduce cost" because managers immediately understand that lowering costs increases their compensation. The final takeaway is, "Reduce cost 15 percent in three steps." (Notice how the supporting slides have takeaways that validate the main one.)

Figure 2-6. Using a Benefit-Driven Takeaway

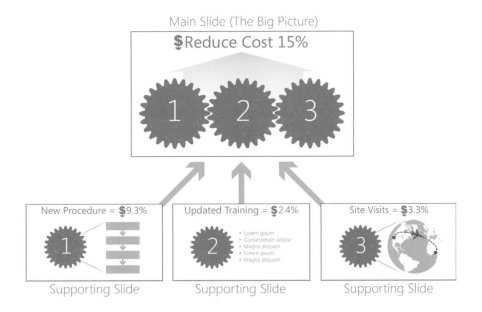

This example shows how the primary takeaway contextualizes and links all slides back to the overall goal, method, and message. When you have statistics that support your takeaway, use them. Quantitative information builds trust; numbers are not needed, but including data gives your audience confidence in your content. Learners intuitively believe that measured content is more likely to be factual.

Tip: For complex explanations, link detailed graphics to an icon of an established overview graphic with a blowout (as shown in Figure 2-6).

Every slide will have a takeaway, a reason to care about that slide. There can be multiple levels of takeaways:

1. The level 1, or primary, takeaway summarizes your entire presentation (or learning document).
2. Level 2 takeaways summarize each slide (or key elements in your document) and support the primary takeaway.
3. Level 3 takeaways support level 2 takeaways.
4. Level 4 takeaways support level 3 takeaways.

The number of levels is dependent upon the size and complexity of your content—there could be a level 5, a level 6, and so on—but all takeaways follow the same rules and support higher-level takeaways. All slides have a takeaway that reinforces your primary takeaway. At the very least, know the takeaway for each slide before you conceptualize it. Start with your primary takeaway and then write your supporting ones.

A primary takeaway is a summary of your entire presentation in one slide. All other levels of takeaways summarize the content on their respective slides and support the primary takeaway in some way. Often, the takeaway appears in the title or is shared verbally by the presenter. Takeaways don't need to be written on your slides, but they must always be understood.

Figure 2-7 demonstrates the relationship between multiple levels of takeaways. Notice how each supports the higher level; all takeaways are interrelated, like Russian nesting dolls.

Summary

Writing a proper takeaway is critical to the success of your presentation. If you fail to define it first, you are doomed to unnecessary revisions. Creating your slides before you know your takeaway is like blindly searching the web without entering search criteria. You may get lucky, but you likely won't find the results you seek. Your takeaway drives the development of your entire presentation.

Here is a best-practice checklist for creating your takeaway:

☐ **Primary takeaway (level 1) written first.**
☐ **Primary takeaway summarizes presentation.**
☐ **Incentivize learner to care.**
☐ **All slides have a takeaway.**
☐ **Higher-level takeaways are supported by lower-level takeaways.**
☐ **One sentence (or two short sentences):**
    ☐ **motivator (pain, gain, fear)**
    ☐ **by what means.**

Figure 2-7. Multiple Levels of Takeaways

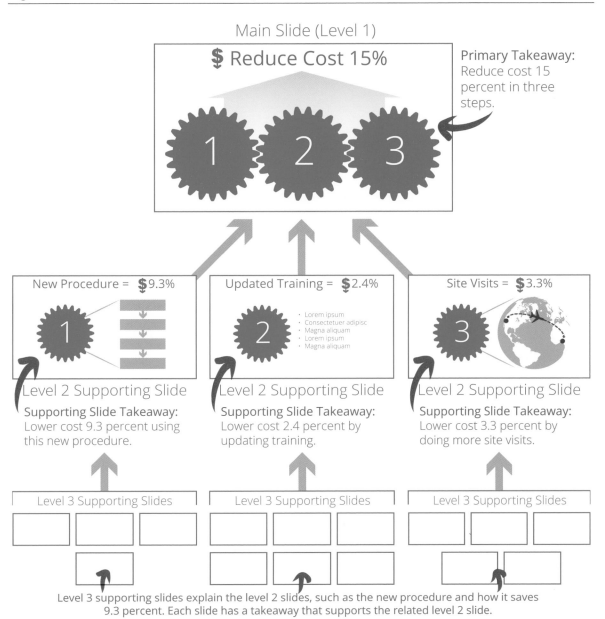

Main Slide (Level 1)

$ Reduce Cost 15%

Primary Takeaway: Reduce cost 15 percent in three steps.

New Procedure = $9.3%

Updated Training = $2.4%
- Lorem ipsum
- Consectetuer adipisc
- Magna aliquam
- Lorem ipsum
- Magna aliquam

Site Visits = $3.3%

Level 2 Supporting Slide

Supporting Slide Takeaway: Lower cost 9.3 percent using this new procedure.

Level 2 Supporting Slide

Supporting Slide Takeaway: Lower cost 2.4 percent by updating training.

Level 2 Supporting Slide

Supporting Slide Takeaway: Lower cost 3.3 percent by doing more site visits.

Level 3 Supporting Slides

Level 3 Supporting Slides

Level 3 Supporting Slides

Level 3 supporting slides explain the level 2 slides, such as the new procedure and how it saves 9.3 percent. Each slide has a takeaway that supports the related level 2 slide.

3

Storyboards for Faster Design

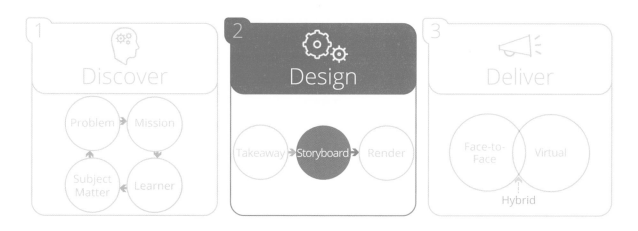

Making your presentation is like building a home. Before you begin construction, you have to draw plans to meet your specific measurements, preferences, and objectives. A successful presentation requires proper planning and a structured approach. Your storyboard is your plan.

To save money and time, directors in the movie industry use storyboards to share actions, framing, pacing, lighting, and a host of other details with the production crew and actors prior to filming. They conceptualize multiple approaches before picking a path forward. You can do the same thing before making your slides.

> "It's not what you want to say, it's what you want to cause."
>
> —Andy Bounds,
> *The Jelly Effect* (2007)

Planning is a critical success factor in any presentation. You may be tempted to first create an outline or slides—but if you do, you are making a presentation for you by you. As I shared before, the reason why most presentations fail is that the authors created it for themselves. The authors based the content and designs on what they wanted to say or see, and not on what their audiences needed to learn to achieve their goals.

Three Keys to Storyboarding

When creating your storyboard, there are three requirements to ensure success:

1. Tell a story.
2. Keep it simple.
3. Use hierarchy and structure.

As the term suggests, your storyboard must tell a story. Stories are proven to activate your learner's brain—conscious and unconscious. Additionally, stories contextualize your content. They connect the dots for the learners and tell them how your slides relate to the takeaway. Expect to use secondary stories within your main story to highlight important points. Graphics and visuals make storytelling easier. For example, I can tell you a story about Sarah's first day at a new company and supplement it with a photograph. Your mind automatically starts to ask questions about the photograph as it pertains to the story, and you start making educated guesses (Figure 3-1).

Figure 3-1. Linking Images to Storytelling

Keep your content succinct; do not add information that isn't germane to your message. Simplifying your content requires a deep understanding of the subject matter. Know your subject matter (see chapter 1), and it will be much easier to explain even the most complex topic in a way that your learner will understand, remember, and apply. Every slide should have a clear, simple message that supports your takeaway. Why include content that is not directly relevant to your message? Also, a properly structured takeaway keeps your audience engaged (see chapter 2). Consider the problem-solving principle known as Ockham's razor: The simplest solution is likely the best. It is applicable to not only your approach, but also how your participants learn. People apply what they understand.

> "Follow the 'one concept per slide' rule. If you have a slide full of bullet points, it's likely that each bullet represents an individual concept. Instead, create an entire section (or subsection) from the slide, turning each bullet into an individual slide that features an insightful headline and a strong supporting graphic."
>
> —Sandra Johnson, Microsoft PowerPoint MVP

Hierarchy and structure deliver your content in an easy-to-follow, intuitive way. These elements make it easy for your audience to connect each slide back to your main takeaway. This approach is no different from writing a book, making a website, or creating an outline.

The Storyboarding Process

Figure 3-2 shows an overview of the storyboarding process. Use it as a starting point and modify it to meet your needs.

Figure 3-2. Process Diagram for Storyboarding

1	2	3	4	5
Outline	Concept and Sketch Slides	Build a Mock Design in PowerPoint	Test	Update

If feedback dictates, update your outline and complete the steps again for those elements that changed.

In step 1, you create an outline based on your primary takeaway. Determine what "buckets" of content are needed to effectively support and explain it. Next, outline the rest of your presentation (or learning document) using supporting takeaways. As with writing, your outline should be hierarchical. Defining these levels makes it easy to create your storyboard. Flesh out as much of your storyboard as possible in this step.

> "Start outside PowerPoint. Write your outline in Word, scribble on Post-its, whatever. Just. Step. Away. From. The. Slide. Once you know what you're going to say, then you can figure out the visuals."
>
> —Echo Swinford, Microsoft PowerPoint MVP

For step 2, you want to conceptualize and sketch your main slide using your primary takeaway as the driver. Sketching helps you make quick choices based on your message and story. Rough drawings coupled with written descriptions speed development and remove aesthetic biases.

Your main slide is a summary of your entire presentation. It does not have to be your first slide, but it should appear early in your deck. This slide becomes your road map. It will be your beginning and (if desired) your conclusion.

Next, sketch your supporting slides using your outline and takeaways as the driver for each slide. Note any animations, videos, imagery, graphics, and audience activities as needed. At this point, use simple annotations to indicate where supplemental materials go.

Conclude with your primary takeaway. This is optional, but this tactic will reinforce your message. Repetition helps your audience remember and believe what you have to say.

Once you are happy with your story, go to step 3. Build simple versions of your slides and use PowerPoint's Slide Sorter and your storyboard view (see the section "Step 3: Build a Mock Design in PowerPoint"). The slides should consist of text, simple notes, and basic PowerPoint procedural graphic elements. Do not spend any time on aesthetic quality, because the more time you spend tweaking aesthetics, the more you become invested in that slide. You are less likely to change it, even if it's necessary.

In step 4, test your mock presentation and collect feedback. Walk through it with either the actual learners or an audience member who is similar to your target learners to get feedback. Share the message for each slide. Ask them if they can follow your story, agree with your messages, and like your approach. Ask for clarification when needed and take notes.

And finally, in step 5, you improve. Once you receive feedback, you rearrange, revise, and edit as needed. If the edits are extensive, go back to step 1 and continue through the storyboarding process for the updated content.

Let's go through each step in greater detail. Tailor what I share to meet your needs.

Step 1: Outline

Great storyboarding is like great writing; the same rules of communication apply. Start with an outline. Chunk your presentation into multiple hierarchical levels—like an outline. Subject matter complexity and duration drives the number of levels needed. For example, a two-day PowerPoint presentation teaching quantum mechanics may require four or more levels. Use as many levels as needed, but remember to keep it simple. It is your job to remove all superfluous data and information and tell the simplest story possible.

The following outline was used to create the storyboard in Figure 3-3.

1. **Reduce cost by 15 percent with three solutions:**
   a. Solution 1: The new procedure reduces cost by 9.3 percent:
      i. Reduce extra work by confirming data are accurate.
      ii. Eliminate two day's work by automating renewal process.
      iii. Avoid collections by automatically sending out a notice.
      iv. Ensure documents are received on time with system confirmations.
   b. Solution 2: Updated training reduces cost by 2.4 percent:
      i. Save $42,000 annually with online training.
      ii. Attendee numbers increase because geography is no longer an issue.
      iii. Faster adoption with less training because the training is more applicable.
      iv. Tests validate understanding.
      v. Recollection is improved through homework.
      vi. Recall is improved with quick reference guides (QRGs).
   c. Solution 3: Site visits reduce cost by 3.3 percent:
      i. Lower the likelihood of production errors with on-site inspections.
      ii. Travel cost is low and return on investment is high.
      iii. Relationships build trust.
      iv. Compliance increases with visit frequency.
      v. There are fewer machine outages because of more visible inspections.
2. **Summary:** Validated that cost reduced by 15 percent with three new solutions.

When first creating your outline and storyboard, expect holes; slides and sections may need more information or thought. Also, expect to struggle with the benefits. Capture what you can and organize in a way that makes sense and is hierarchical, then go back and refine it.

Figure 3-3 shows a multilevel hierarchical structure, following the outline, to create an easy-to-follow storyboard that educates learners. An effective strategy is to begin and end with your primary takeaway, which shares what the learner will get. The rest of the slides explain how they will get it, and your conclusion reminds them of your initial promise—the primary takeaway. For example, the primary takeaway is "Reduce cost 15 percent in three steps." You conclude with something like, "And now you see how the three steps reduce cost 15 percent." Concluding with your primary takeaway is optional and is at your discretion.

Figure 3-3. Storyboard Based on the Outline

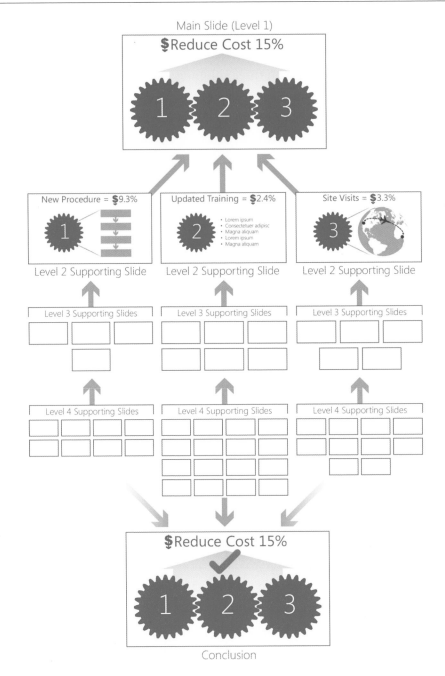

There are other storyboard structures, but they all require an outline to guarantee a cohesive, logical flow to your narrative. In testing different structures over the last 15 years, I have found that the hierarchical structure can be applied to most presentations.

After you have mastered the hierarchical structure, experiment with others. Learn what is best for your audience, subject matter, and (if you are presenting) your natural speaking style. Figure 3-4 shows four flow charts that represent additional storyboard structures. They're ideal for presentations intended to entertain, persuade, or motivate, such as giving to a charity, team building, or selling a service. The boxes can represent multiple slides.

Figure 3-4. Types of Storyboard Structures

Inspiration Structure
Repeats as Needed
As Is (Challenges) → To Be (Solutions) → Call to Action → Goal State (After Solutions Applied)

Resolution Structure
Problem → Potential Solution 1 / Potential Solution 2 / Potential Solution N → Chosen Solution → Why? (Include Benefits)

Story Structure
Set the Stage and Introduce the Challenge → Introduce the Hero → Introduce the Complication → Resulting Crisis → Hero Resolves Crisis

Wow Structure
New, Surprising, or Shocking Solution → Benefits of New Solution → Loss of Not Implementing Solution (Optional) → Call to Action to Implement New Solution

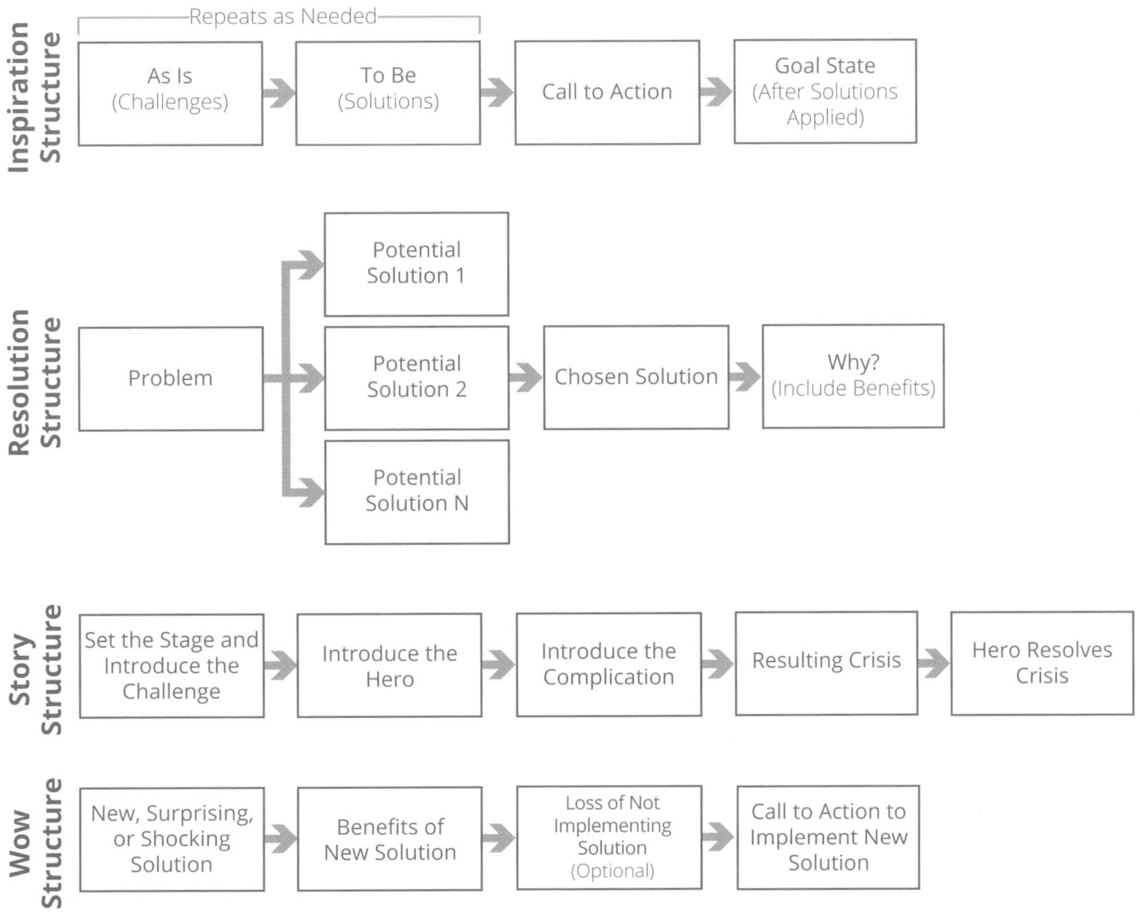

For historical and time-based stories, also consider the chronological structure (Figure 3-5).

Figure 3-5. Chronological Storyboard Structure

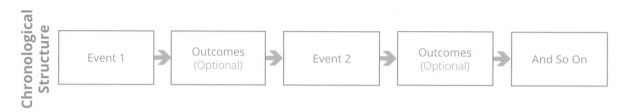

For larger, more complex presentations, consider using visual cues to orient your audience. In Figure 3-6, tabs organize and present the content. Be creative and use a visual approach that is intuitive and complements your subject matter. (See the appendix for graphical suggestions.)

Figure 3-6. Using Tabs as Visual Cues

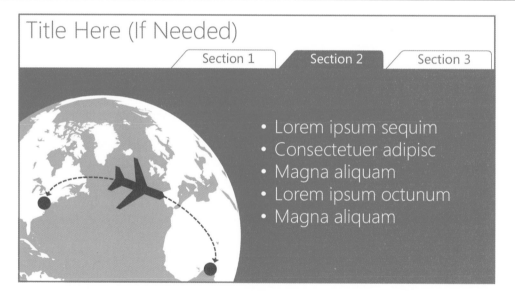

Step 2: Conceptualize and Sketch Slides

I am often asked, "How many slides should I aim for?" A lot of variables determine the total slide count, such as subject matter, audience expectation, content, takeaways, delivery method, and the presenter's speaking style. If a total slide estimate is needed before beginning, divide the total duration into one- to 10-minute chunks, depending on your style of speaking. Each chunk equals a slide. If it's a fast-paced presentation, assume a slide per minute. If it's slower-paced, assume one slide for every five or 10 minutes. I have seen a slide per second and a slide per hour. Never include slides to fill time or delete critical content to save time. Find better ways to share the information to fit into the allotted timeframe.

["If you can't explain it simply, you don't understand it well enough."

—Albert Einstein]

Most learners are resource starved, and their attention is fractured. When you have control over duration, keep it short. What is the fastest, most effective way to achieve the objectives? For example, when I taught solution architecture to a team of PhDs, I delivered a 10-minute PowerPoint presentation and a PowerPoint infographic. I storyboarded both the presentation and infographic the same way. The supporting elements in the infographic were conceptualized as if they were slides (Figure 3-7).

Figure 3-7. Storyboard for a PowerPoint Infographic

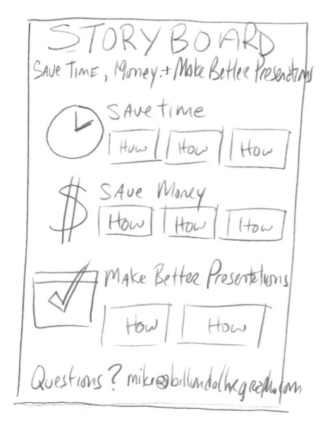

The secret when storyboarding is to move fast and be agile. You want to have no initial investment in one solution. To ensure this, I sketch my storyboard with a paper and pencil. (You can also do the same with an electronic tablet and writing device.) It's much faster to draw the storyboard first, because you don't get duped into determining aesthetics early in the process. As soon as you use PowerPoint, there is a desire to make it aesthetically appealing from the start and play around with repositioning elements, changing colors, and wordsmithing. These actions waste your valuable time and are counterproductive when storyboarding.

You want to quickly block out what each slide communicates when sketching graphic ideas. You don't have to be Leonardo da Vinci. Your objective is to capture your thoughts quickly so you can move forward and evolve your storyboard—your plan. Tell your story with slides the way you would tell a story with friends. Be fluid and conversational. The faster you lay it out, the less invested you are. And the less invested you are, the more willing you are to alter your storyboard when you find a better way. This approach improves creativity; you are brainstorming potential paths forward.

I used the following storyboard (Figure 3-8) to create the PowerPoint presentation for ATD's Essential Series PowerPoint class. The final slide shown in this storyboard is my main slide—my primary takeaway.

Figure 3-8. Storyboard Sketch

Note ideas for images, graphics, animations, exercises, and supporting materials by jotting them down under the slide. Use this approach to build your PowerPoint learning materials. For example, in the storyboard for the PowerPoint infographic (Figure 3-7), I used the takeaway—save time and money, and make better presentations, by storyboarding—to craft the title and the infographic's content. Everything connects to and supports my takeaway.

Tip: To get ideas for learner exercises that support your messages, search online for "educational exercises," "training exercises," "team-building activities," or "learning activities." You will a find sea of options ranging from group activities to role playing to games. Weave these phrases into your storyboard, as needed, with simple notes.

Expect to sketch multiple options to show potential solutions. If you focus on one solution before considering alternatives, you may overlook a better path forward. PowerPoint gurus generate different options before uncovering the best solution for their audience.

Review each storyboard option. Does it support your takeaway? Does it tell a story? Is it engaging? If yes, move forward. Reject approaches that do not meet your needs. In my experience, you will know the right solution because everything logically fits. Your topics and takeaways suddenly come together like puzzle pieces.

When planning your presentation, remember that great PowerPoint is a dialogue with your learners, not a monologue. Your presentation should always involve the learner. It is a discussion with your audience. If you construct your takeaway the way I shared, the learner will extrinsically or intrinsically ask two questions: "What?" and "How?"

For example, if your takeaway is, "Go home earlier using the new automated system," your participants will want to know, "What is the new automated system?" and "How will it help me go home earlier?" Your job is to answer what and how within your content. When a learner asks a conscious or unconscious question, they are engaged.

For presentations, use cognitive curiosity to further engage your audience. Cognitive curiosity evokes the underlying motivation in learners to seek more information through investigation. To do so, keep your learner guessing. As soon as your audience thinks they know what you are going to say, do, or show, their minds will automatically tune out, and they'll be distracted by competing thoughts. For this reason, I rarely include titles on my slides, and when I do, it's a motivator, as described in chapter 2. I don't want my class to know what I'm going to say before I say it.

You want the learners' minds to constantly ask questions to receive the next reward. If you give their unconscious minds a puzzle to solve with a reward, they are compelled to pay attention. The unconscious (and possibly conscious) mind is driven to figure it out. Use metaphors, slow reveals with stories, and things that are incongruent with what is expected—sometimes referred to as cognitive dissonance. Your learners' minds try to understand where you are going and become connected with you and the content.

Our learners' unconscious minds love safe surprises. You've heard the saying, "Content is king"—it isn't. Contrast is king. Your audience pays more attention to things that are unusual. The reason human brains are wired this way is because things that are different are more likely to hurt us than things that are the same. Have you ever walked into a room and forgotten why you entered the room in the first place? That's because our unconscious mind automatically purges our short-term memory to take in the new environment. We were safe in the previous room, but there could be danger in a new room. Our mind is looking for things that are incongruent with what we expect to see, hear, feel, or smell. If we do sense something out of the ordinary, our subconscious quickly gets to work at solving the puzzle. Within nanoseconds, our brain asks, "What is it? Can it hurt me? What does it mean? What should I do?" Our learners' brains are wired to react this way to things that are different.

> You've heard the saying, "Content is king"—it isn't. Contrast is king.

It is unlikely that you want your audience to be afraid. For this reason, make sure your "surprises" (evoking cognitive curiosity) are safe and nonthreatening. Tactics that can create cognitive curiosity and safe surprises include:

- metaphors
- analogies
- similes
- odd sounds
- stories
- unique graphics or aesthetics
- incongruent photographs
- unfamiliar videos
- unpredictable animations.

Another approach is to use cognitive dissonance, which is defined as having inconsistent thoughts, beliefs, or attitudes. For our purposes, it means doing or showing something unexpected. To qualify your safe surprises and cognitive dissonance as educational, they must be relevant. Suddenly using an air horn during your class may startle your participants, but it becomes a distraction if it has no relevance to your topic. Shocking your audience to grab their attention with no payout will disrupt the learning process.

One cognitive curiosity technique is to slowly reveal your content. For example, imagine a PowerPoint presentation for employees at a pharmaceutical company. The presentation is meant to advance the organization using this takeaway: "Improve the quality of our solutions by merging the product development and services divisions." An animation or a build

> Tip: Aesthetically unique ways of showing information hold your audience's attention, increase retention, and amplify their emotional response. For example, do you remember seeing groundbreaking special effects in a movie? How did it make you feel? However, do not sacrifice communication for innovation. It is better to be predictable and clear than clever and confusing.

that reveals a DNA graphic metaphor employs effective cognitive curiosity and is a safe surprise. It is unexpected. At first, the audience is unaware of the full message and visual metaphor. As time goes by, the metaphor and its relevance is revealed, accompanied by a story. Figure 3-9 is a three-slide example showing the DNA metaphor build. The narrative appears beneath each slide.

Figure 3-9. DNA Graphic Animation

"How do we achieve better solutions? The first step involves our product development division. This division has amazing R&D and execution strategies. Staff and consumer insight can be improved."

"The second step requires the strength of our services division, with efficient staffing and consumer access."

"Combining these two complementary divisions gives us the DNA of the new, improved PDS division. Now, let me explain how this will work. . . ."

Subtle, simple aesthetic choices work, too. Figure 3-10 is a divider slide that uses minimalism, white space, and layout as a safe surprise. The large orange circle hangs off the left side of the slide and flirts with space around the page.

Figure 3-10. Using Minimalism

A presentation is meant to be a visual medium, whereas most printed material focuses on the words. When developing ideas for your slides, think visually. Text is acceptable in small amounts; not everything should be a visual. If everything were a graphic, your graphics would have less power. Use graphics for those ideas that warrant additional attention. Do not use graphics as aesthetic embellishment.

I work with government contractors to develop oral proposals. Most of the time, graphics are added as an afterthought to text-heavy slides because the presentation looks boring (according to the authors themselves). The graphics they add are not created for that slide. Instead, graphics are added because they found an image with a tangential relationship to something on their slide. Usually, it is an old proposal graphic, an image the author found online (which is likely illegal to use in a proposal), or a PowerPoint graphic element. The end result is a text-heavy slide with confusing, unprofessional, or illegible images. The slide's effectiveness is diminished, not enhanced. The government's evaluation

> Research shows that presentations using visual aids are 43 percent more persuasive than unaided presentations (Vogel, Dickson, and Lehman 1986).

of the solution provider is negatively affected and, as a result, the likelihood of winning the contract is poor at best.

There are three reasons to use a graphic in a presentation:

1. It is a critical success factor.
2. It is too complex to understand textually.
3. It supports a specific emotional message.

The critical success factor is any content that, if missed or misunderstood, would result in a failure to learn. In other words, if your audience misses this key point, your PowerPoint content would be ineffective.

When words alone are not enough to communicate a concept, use a graphic. For example, imagine trying to educate your learners on the organizational structure of a large company. Why use only text when you can show an organizational chart? Or perhaps there is a complex process to understand. Imagine trying to learn how to tie a tie through a textual description versus a step-by-step diagram (Figure 3-11). Which directions are easier to understand and apply?

> Do not use graphics as aesthetic embellishment. Deliberately choose visual elements that improve communication and support your goals.

Figure 3-11. Text Description or Step-by-Step Diagram?

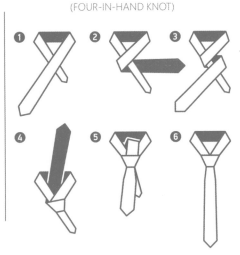

> "Use the storyboarding add-in from Visual Studio (or download the Team Foundation Server Office Integration 2017 to get the add-in) to save and reuse your own custom shapes and gradient overlays. It has saved me so much time."
>
> —Heather Ackmann, Microsoft PowerPoint MVP

Images are great when eliciting a specific emotional response. For example, our audience likes to see themselves reflected in our materials. It increases trust. To build that trust, I may show photographs of familiar people, places, or things.

Don't confuse a graphical element, such as a line or PowerPoint template parts, with a graphic. A graphical element separates, highlights, or identifies pieces of your content and your brand. A graphic is a visual representation of an idea, meant to clarify and explain.

When creating ideas for visuals, refer to the graphic types in the appendix. Every slide, infographic, or visual you'll make conveys one of these concepts: amount or value, architecture or structure, cause and effect, comparison, hierarchy, location or distance, physical description, process or flow, protection or isolation, relationship, synergy, time, or transition. Once you know the concept, pick the graphic type that clearly communicates your story.

Once you have finished the first draft of your storyboard, then refine, evolve, and improve it. Hand drawing your storyboard enables you to easily sketch new ideas, erase those that aren't relevant, and rearrange the storyline—before you render slides in PowerPoint. When you follow this technique, you should only need to lay out your slides once within the package and save time making endless revisions and redesigning graphics.

Step 3: Build a Mock Design in PowerPoint

Now it's time to build a prototype in PowerPoint—a mock-up of your slides. Use descriptions in lieu of creating graphics, photographs, videos, or animations. A prototype allows you to click through your ideas and experience the flow and pacing. It gives you an opportunity to test your PowerPoint content and determine if it meets your expectations before rendering the final slides. Use PowerPoint's Slide Sorter view to update and rearrange your content as needed based on feedback.

> Tip: For some versions of PowerPoint, type *=lorem()* and hit return to get placeholder text.

The basic principle behind storyboarding is breaking your presentation into bite-sized chunks and reassembling those morsels to tell a compelling narrative. Your slides are the ingredients, and your storyboard is the recipe—the architecture for your presentation.

Step 4: Test

What would happen if you spent days, weeks, or months making your presentation, only to have it not meet your objectives once delivered? How would you feel? Always find a way to test your PowerPoint storyboard before settling on a final design. When possible, once you have your potential solution, ask your learners, or seek out friends who are similar to your target audience. Walk them through it. What do they think? Collect their feedback and update if needed.

Tip: Use sections to organize your slides. (Think of them as folders for your slides.) To add a section, go to Normal or Slide Sorter view. Next, select the slide that you want to be first in your new section. On the Home tab, click the Section button and click Add Section.

Based on my experience, and the experience of other presenters, your presentation will be successful if you rigorously test the content.

Step 5: Update

Nothing is perfect. There is always room for improvement. When you receive feedback, no matter how difficult to hear, evaluate it and choose to incorporate or discard it. If the corrective recommendations are extensive, go back to step 1.

When I receive feedback, there are often one to three major changes, and the rest are minor updates. The more you do it, the fewer edits you can expect.

Summary

Your storyboard is your plan. Do not jump ahead. Always plan first. When authors jump into PowerPoint without outlining or sketching ideas, it takes them longer to produce a deliverable of high quality, and the end product is less effective.

Here is a best practice checklist for developing your storyboard:

- ☐ **Create your outline first.**
- ☐ **Conceptualize and sketch slides.**
- ☐ **Use visuals and activities to engage.**
- ☐ **Tell a story and view your content as a dialogue.**
- ☐ **For presentations, use cognitive dissonance.**
- ☐ **Include safe surprises.**
- ☐ **Build a mock design in PowerPoint.**
- ☐ **Test your content.**
- ☐ **Update as needed based on feedback.**

4

Render: PowerPoint Tips, Tricks, and Secrets

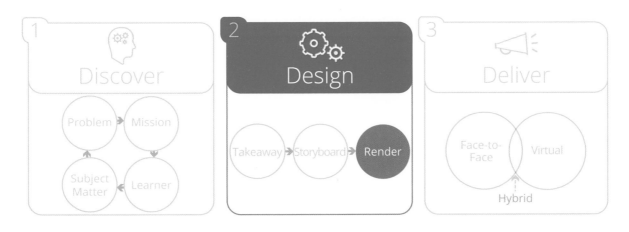

The quality of your presentation represents the quality of your content. If your slides, visuals, or supplemental PowerPoint files look unprofessional and are peppered with grammatical and spelling errors, the perceived value of your content goes down. For this reason, render your slides using the guidelines outlined in this chapter and always check your work. When possible, ask a colleague to do a QC (quality control) pass. Find any elements that may be seen as unprofessional and fix them before presenting your slides to your learners. Professionalism improves the likelihood of adoption.

> "It was a revelation to discover how design could . . . change people's behavior. I learned that simply by altering the graphic content of an exhibit you could double the number of people who visited."
>
> —Gillian Thomas, Formerly of The Science Museum/UK (Peters 2005)

Rendering refers to making your slides (and other learning materials) in PowerPoint. It includes text, layout, formatting, templates, colors, fonts, photographs, graphics, icons, symbols, animations, video, sound, and interactivity. To be proficient, you must understand how to design your materials in PowerPoint, and why you should spend time creating them.

When learners see your content, they initially react to its look and feel, such as color, style, and imagery. You want to control their first impression. Different aesthetic choices cause different responses in learners, so understanding these variables is important. The styles you choose communicate information about the content and presenter.

Trends come and go. For example, several years ago, skeuomorphism was the preferred style—graphics that try to mimic reality using tricks with design elements like gradients, drop shadows, and bevels. Recently, designers have turned to flat and linear designs, which eliminate most aesthetic embellishments in favor of simplicity (Figure 4-1). Applying skeuomorphism to graphics in a presentation for Millennials (who are used to the modern, flat graphic style) may cause them to view your information as outdated.

Figure 4-1. Graphic Styles

Have you seen a design you liked? What specifically did you like about it? It could be the colors, style, photographic imagery, lighting, or typeface. Keep a journal of designs you like. If something inspires you, download it, take a photograph, or clip it from a magazine, and save it to a creativity folder.

Know how your learners will react to your choices: Ask them. Ask someone like them. Make an educated guess. Do not let your personal biases support aesthetic choices that may negatively affect your learners' perceptions of your PowerPoint slides and materials. For example, I was creating a presentation for a state university, and my point of contact was tired of seeing their brand colors, so she wanted to use a different color palette. The presentation's objective was to educate businesses on the

> Tip: The rendering style should be consistent with the audience, subject matter, and the emotions you want to elicit. Avoid amateur aesthetics and avoid making a bad first impression.

university's continuing education programs and certifications. In the end, we created a fantastic presentation that failed to brand the university. When the audience recalled the presentation, it was confused with a competing college. The institution lost an opportunity to build brand recognition through repeated, consistent exposure. My point of contact's bias kept her from making an objective decision that aligned with the presentation's goals.

Key PowerPoint Functions

To render professional PowerPoint slides, you want to know the key PowerPoint functions and design principles. Everything is interrelated; nothing exists in a vacuum (Figure 4-2).

Figure 4-2. PowerPoint Functions Are Interrelated

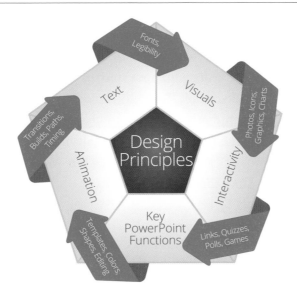

PowerPoint is a robust tool. This book includes many of the features I use most—features that help you render quality presentations fast. Here are the key tools covered in this book:

- Themes
- Slide Master and Notes Pages
- Sections
- Shapes (Format Shape)
- Align and Distribute Objects
- Reorder Objects
- Merge (or Combine) Shapes
- Color
- Text and Text Format
- Slide Size
- Format Painter
- Charts
- SmartArt
- Animation
- Transitions
- Interactivity (Hyperlink, Action)
- Insert Pictures, Video, and Audio
- Editing Pictures, Video, and Audio
- Resolution
- Exporting and Sharing (File Types)
- Grouping
- Recording.

"Use right-click (or control-click for Mac) to easily access menu options."

—Glenna Shaw,
Microsoft PowerPoint MVP

Note that the following instructions and screenshots apply to Microsoft PowerPoint 2016 for Windows, the latest version at the time of publication. The platform may change in future versions.

Themes

Using a custom theme helps ensure your slides are unique, consistent, easier to build, and faster to edit. A theme defines the default appearance of your PowerPoint content. It indicates your colors, fonts, effects, and background. Every PowerPoint document is governed by a theme. Setting up and following your theme makes it easy to change layouts, colors, fonts, and other design elements, while improving the perceived professionalism of your presentation.

You can choose one of Microsoft's themes in the Design tab. Modify it, as needed, and save it as your theme (name it) for use in your other PowerPoint files.

Here's how to apply a theme:

1. Display in Normal view.
2. To select a theme, go to the Design tab and click the More button (arrow down) in the Themes group. View the Office theme gallery and any custom templates on your computer. (Place your cursor over a theme thumbnail for a preview.) Click a theme to apply it.
3. To change colors, go to the Design tab. Click the More button (arrow down) in the Variants group and select Colors. Click the color set to apply it. To customize the

colors, choose Customize Colors at the bottom of the Colors drop-down menu
(Figure 4-3).

4. To change fonts, go to the Design tab, click the More button (arrow down) in the
   Variants group, and select Fonts. Click the font set you want to apply. To customize
   the fonts, select Customize Fonts at the bottom of the Fonts drop-down menu.

5. To change effects, go to the Design tab. Click the More button (arrow down) in the
   Variants group and click Effects. Click the effect style you want to apply.

6. To change the background, go to the Design tab. Click the More button (arrow down)
   in the Variants group and click Background Styles. Click the background to apply
   it. To customize your background, select Format Background at the bottom of the
   Background Styles drop-down menu.

Figure 4-3. Screenshot of PowerPoint Themes

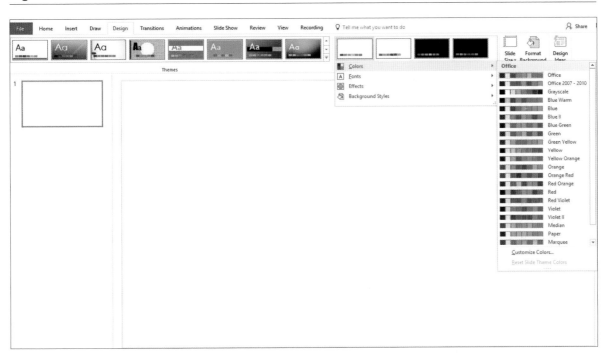

Slide Master and Notes Pages

The PowerPoint Slide Master is a template—a series of customizable layouts from which to choose
based on your needs. Your document can have multiple templates, but for most presentations I

Tip: At any time, you can save your theme by clicking Save Current Theme, which is located in the Slide Master tab under the Themes drop-down menu.

recommend one. For the casual user, having more than one Slide Master increases the likelihood of errors due to complexity. To access the Slide Master, go to the View tab and select Slide Master (Figure 4-4).

Figure 4-4. Slide Master

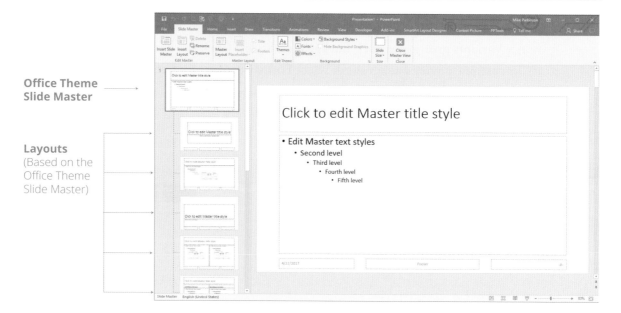

A Slide Master comprises an Office Theme Slide Master (the main layout) and corresponding layouts. Modifications to the main layout affect the corresponding layouts. For more complex presentations with multiple presenters or styles, you can have more than one Office Theme Slide Master. For example, if you have a presentation with different, distinct topics, you may want a different Slide Master for each. I have not used this approach, but know many others who have.

Format your layouts by repositioning or changing text boxes, or by adding a background, graphic elements, or images. Each default layout—for example, Title and Content Layout or Title Slide Layout—is applicable to different needs. Layouts can be added, deleted, repositioned, edited, and renamed (right-click the layout you want to rename and select Rename Layout).

To apply a Slide Master layout to your presentations, go to the Home tab and select Layout. Pick your preferred layout. Like styles in Word, modifying any of the Slide Master layouts affects all slides in your deck that use that layout.

To ensure that your audience is not reading your slides and ignoring you, avoid putting all of your text on your slides. Instead, share your Notes Pages. You can format your individual Notes Pages as if they were Word pages (Figure 4-5). You can edit and brand, and add more text, new graphics, and other elements as desired. The text that automatically appears under your slide is your speaker notes. Modify your speaker notes to act as your reference material. To access your Notes Pages, go to the View tab and select Notes Page. Print or save your Notes Pages, which include your slides, as a leave behind.

"Learn to customize the PowerPoint ribbon and menus. It is your application; make the commands display in the way you want them to, the way they make sense to you!"

—Ric Bretschneider,
Microsoft PowerPoint MVP

Figure 4-5. Formatted and Modified Notes Page

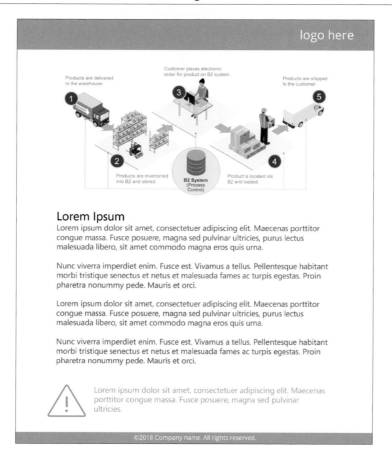

Sections

Sections keep your slides organized. Consider them as folders for your slides, which are grouped by the section titles, as seen in Figure 4-6. They only appear in Normal and Slide Sorter views. Sections do not affect the flow of your presentation.

To apply a section, go to the Normal or Slide Sorter view. Next, select the slide that you want as the first one in your new section. On the Home tab, click the Section button and choose Add Section. To rename, right-click the section title you want to edit and select Rename Section.

Figure 4-6. PowerPoint Sections Are Like Folders for Your Slides

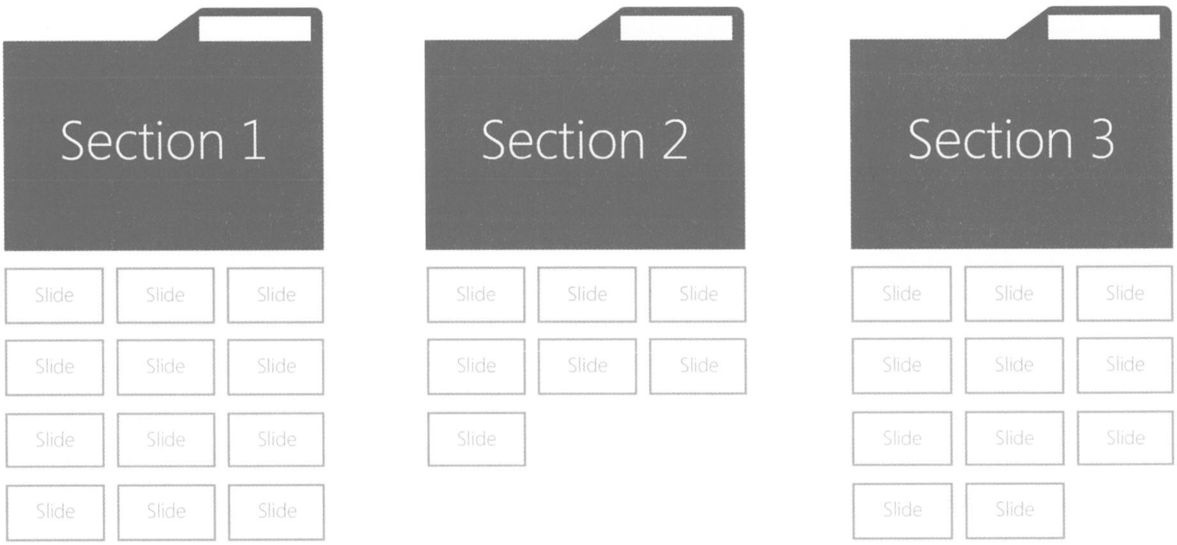

Shapes

PowerPoint offers many basic shapes from which to choose. Shapes are essential design tools for two main reasons:

- Placing your content into shapes helps chunk your content.
- Any graphic imaginable can be made from default PowerPoint shapes using Merge Shapes.

To access shapes, go to the Insert tab and select Shapes. Draw the shape on your slide. To change your shape's appearance, select it and right-click. Choose Format Shape. From there you can edit your shape's fill, outline, effects, size, and properties.

The Format Shape option lets you customize your objects. For example, you can change the fill color and outline colors (Table 4-1).

Table 4-1. Customizing Fill and Line Options

Fill	Line
• **No fill** (no fill color) • **Solid fill** (one fill color) • **Gradient fill** (gradated fill color—pick the number of colors and position of each) • **Picture or texture fill** (fill with a picture or preloaded texture) • **Pattern fill** (fill with a preloaded pattern) • **Slide background fill** (background fill) • **Color** (defines fill colors) • **Transparency** (defines fill opacity)	• **No line** (no outline) • **Solid line** (has an outline) • **Gradient line** (gradated outline color—pick the number of colors and position of each) • **Color** (defines outline colors) • **Transparency** (defines fill opacity) • **Gradient** (pick gradient colors and position) • **Line Effects** (compound lines, dashed lines, cap and join styles, arrow heads)

Use solid, "flat" colors to make shapes look modern, simple, and clean. Use a gradient fill to make your objects look more realistic. Gradients consist of "stops"; each stop is a color you choose. You can add or delete stops as needed to achieve the desired effect. Selecting the Rotate with shape option locks your gradient orientation to your shape's rotation.

Under Format Shape, you can also add one or more of the following effects by selecting Shape Effects (the names may change slightly based on the version of PowerPoint you use):

- **Drop Shadow:** Adds a formatted shadow to an object
- **Reflection:** Looks as if your object is mirrored in a reflective surface
- **Glow:** Allows you to add a halo of color around your object
- **Soft Edges:** Blurs the edges of your object
- **3-D Rotation:** Rotates your object in three-dimensional space
- **3-D Format and Bevel:** Adds an edge, shaped contour, and/or extrudes your object in three-dimensional space.

Always use effects that add value and not because you think they look cool. All aesthetic choices should have a reason for being selected, one that supports your goals.

The following is a high-level explanation of the three-dimensional features found in PowerPoint: With 3-D Format, you can change your object's bevel size and type, extend it in three-dimensional space (the Z axis), and modify the look and feel (Figure 4-7). For bevels, select a predefined contour and change the width and height. Top Bevel refers to the front-facing slide of your object. Bottom Bevel is the opposite side. Depth extrudes your object into the Z axis. Size refers to the distance between the front and back faces of your object. Contour defines your object's edge color. (Surface) Material and Lighting options affect the shading, color, and transparency of your object—depending upon which option you choose.

Figure 4-7. Using Bevels

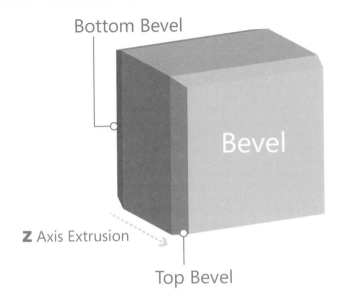

The 3-D Rotation options rotate a selected object in three-dimensional space. When rotating the object, you can choose between the preset rotation options or numeric rotations. Preset rotations are broken into parallel, perspective, and oblique sets. Parallel rotation has no vanishing point; therefore, objects with the same rotation can easily fit together, like building blocks. Perspective rotation mimics reality with a vanishing point. Objects with a perspective rotation will not fit together due to the vanishing point. Objects rotated using the oblique set follow the same rules as the parallel rotation option (Figure 4-8).

Using numeric fields, you can change the X, Y, and Z axes' rotation (also known as roll, pitch, and yaw, respectively) of an object. Figure 4-9 shows the axis about which your object is rotated.

All basic shapes are made of points (vertices). These points can be edited. Edit Points allows you to sculpt PowerPoint shapes and change their form. To access this feature, select your shape on the Format tab, choose Edit Shape, and click Edit Points. The points that make up your shape are now visible. Select and move either the vertex (black point) or the handle (white points at the end of the blue handle bar) to modify your shape (Figure 4-10).

Figure 4-8. Perspective and Oblique Rotations

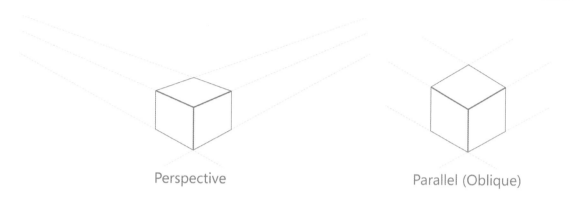

Perspective   Parallel (Oblique)

Figure 4-9. Rotating or Extruding an Object in X, Y, and Z Axes

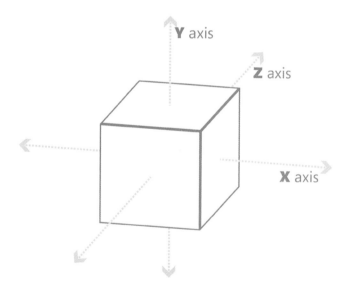

Figure 4-10. Modifying a Figure's Shape

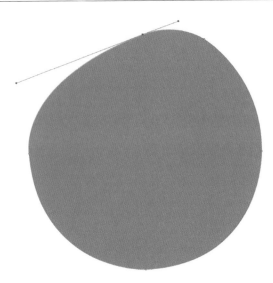

Format Shape also gives you the ability to format size, proportions, and position. Most notable in this section is formatting the text box. You can change things like:

- vertical alignment (where your text appears within the object)
- text direction (changes the direction of your text within your object)
- how your shape is affected by text (for example, you can "autofit" text, shrink text to stay within your object, or resize your object to accommodate the text)
- text margins (changes the proximity of text with the edge of your object).

As with all functionality, play with PowerPoint's options and watch the changes within your shape to learn what each feature does.

Align and Distribute Objects

Aligning and evenly distributing objects denotes professionalism. For example, use this function to keep your flowchart boxes aligned and spaced evenly.

To align objects, select what you want to align (hold the Shift key to select multiple objects). Under the Home tab, select Arrange, and then select Align. Choose from Align Left, Align Center, Align Right, Align Top, Align Middle, and Align Bottom.

To evenly distribute your objects, hold down the Shift key and select three or more objects. Go to the Home tab, select Arrange, and then Distribute Horizontally or Distribute Vertically. Doing so automatically makes your objects equidistant from one another—no guessing required.

Reorder Objects

All elements on your slide exist on different layers or planes—one in front of the other. To reorder the elements on a slide, select an object. Go to the Home tab and choose Arrange. From there, you will find several options: Bring to Front, Send to Back, Bring Forward, or Send Backward. Consider using this function for slides with overlapping objects or complex layouts. Grouping objects automatically places all selected objects on the same layer (Figure 4-11).

Figure 4-11. Understanding Layers

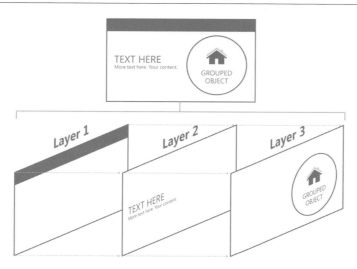

Merge (or Combine) Shapes

Using Merge Shapes, you can add or subtract shapes to an existing one. With this function, you can construct any graphic you can imagine. To use Merge Shapes, select two overlapping shapes (hold your Shift key to select two shapes). Under the Format tab, select Merge Shapes. The order in which you select the shapes affects the final outcome, because the shape you select first becomes the primary shape. For example, if you select two squares and you choose Subtract, the first square is subtracted from the second one. Figure 4-12 illustrates how each Merge Shapes feature works.

> "On Windows, use Selection Pane (Alt + F10) to quickly access elements on your slide. To access it, go to the Editing area on your Home tab and choose Selection Pane from the Select menu options."
>
> —John Wilson,
> Microsoft PowerPoint MVP

Figure 4-12. Using Merge Shapes

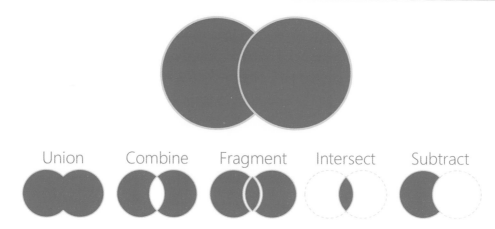

Format and combine shapes to make professional, complex PowerPoint native images. Creating the graphics in PowerPoint will make it easier for you and others on your team to edit the graphics. The diagrams in appendix B provide step-by-step instructions to create several widely used and recognized graphic metaphors in PowerPoint: a gear, a funnel, a gauge, and a conveyor belt.

Explore the powerful Merge Shapes tool. Give yourself a project: Find a graphic you like and re-create it. Look at an object and break it into basic shapes that can be created with Merge Shapes. Use the step-by-step examples in appendix B for inspiration and become comfortable making custom PowerPoint graphics.

Color

In most versions of PowerPoint, you have four ways to modify colors:

1. **Grayscale:** A gradient of white to black. Grayscale is focused on value, or how light or dark the color is.

2. **RGB:** All colors can be described as percentages of red, green, and blue. RGB is most often used.

3. **CMYK:** All colors can be described as percentages of cyan, magenta, yellow, and black. (Black is the "key" color, hence the *K*.) CMYK is used most for printed documents because printers use corresponding color cartridges to build colors.

4. **HSL (or HSB):** All colors can be described on the hue, saturation, or luminosity spectrum. (*B* refers to brightness.) HSL is my preferred choice, because it is more intuitive to modify the variables that make up any given color. Hue is where a color

appears on the rainbow (for example, yellow versus blue). Saturation is how intense or vibrant a color is (pastel versus neon). Luminosity, or value, is how light or dark a color is (adding white or black to change value).

Text and Text Format

To add text, insert a text box and begin typing. To modify, go to the Home tab, where you can change fonts, text styles, text colors, and more in the Font group. Change line and paragraph spacing by selecting the Paragraph drop-down menu in the lower-right corner of the Paragraph Group on the Home tab.

> Tip: Change the spacing around the text within a shape or text box under Format Shape. Select Size and Properties and then Text Box. There, you can change your left, right, top, and bottom margins.

Slide Size

PowerPoint isn't limited to presentations. It can be used to make other learning materials such as handouts, infographics, cheat sheets, and assessments. Tailor your slide (page) size by clicking on the Design tab, choose Slide Size, and select Custom Slide Size (or Page Setup). Change the width and height to your desired dimensions.

You will then have the option of scaling or not scaling your content to the new size. The choice is yours, but if the aspect ratio changes (relative width or height), your images will be distorted—either stretched or squished to fit.

Due to the aspect ratio of your laptop, monitors, displays, and smart devices, 16:9 (13.33 inches by 7.5 inches) is considered a current, or modern, slide size (Figure 4-13).

Figure 4-13. Working With Aspect Ratio

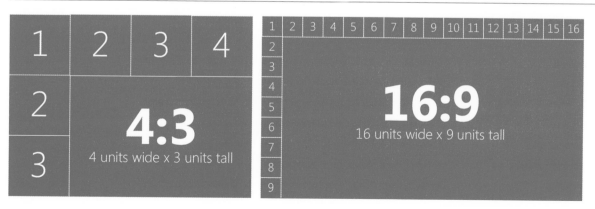

Change the dimensions of your PowerPoint file to meet your needs. For example, if you are making an infographic, choose a size that works best for the medium on which it will be presented.

Format Painter

To improve consistency, use the Format Painter to sample and apply styles such as font type, size, and color. To use, select the object from which you want to sample a style. On the Home tab, click Format Painter (or Format). Click on the object to which you want to apply the sampled style.

Tip: Double-click Format Painter to retain the sampled style and apply it to multiple objects. Click Escape to release the sampled style.

Charts

PowerPoint charts are an efficient way to present quantitative information. To add a chart, click on the Insert tab and select Chart. Choose a chart type and then double-click the chart style you want. Replace the default data in PowerPoint's spreadsheet with your information. Close the spreadsheet to apply your data.

Use Table 4-2 to select the best chart for your needs.

Table 4-2. PowerPoint Chart Types

Chart Type	Best To
Column and Bar	Compare changes over time for one or a few quantitative elements
Line	Compare changes over time for one to many quantitative elements
Pie	Compare quantitative parts to a whole
Area	Compare changes over time for one or a few quantitative elements
XY (Scatter)	Show correlations between the values of quantities
Stock	Analyze movements of a security, derivative, or currency in the market
Surface	Show the connection of data points through pattern recognition
Radar	Compare quantitative elements with three or more scales
Treemap	Compare relative data amounts in the form of nested rectangles
Sunburst	Compare hierarchical proportions depicted by concentric circles
Histogram	Compare quantitative amounts for data ranges
Box and Whisker	Analyze the distribution of a dataset
Waterfall	Analyze the cumulative effect of sequential values

In Microsoft Excel, eliminate or hide data from your PowerPoint chart by resizing the bounding box using the lower right corner (Figure 4-14). To add elements, increase the size of the bounding box to accommodate a new series. PowerPoint automatically syncs with and seamlessly works through Excel for chart data. Renaming content in Excel changes content in PowerPoint.

Figure 4-14. Resizing PowerPoint Data With Excel

A	B	C	D
	Series 1	Series 2	Series 3
Category 1	4.3	2.4	2
Category 2	2.5	4.4	2
Category 3	3.5	1.8	3
Category 4	4.5	2.8	5

Resize in Excel to remove or add data elements in your PowerPoint chart.

Click within your chart to manipulate colors and line styles and delete or move the legend. To edit data after making your graphic, right-click on the chart and select Edit Data. For more editing options, go to the Design tab and review the Add Chart Element options. Test a few functions and observe the results. To change your chart type, click Change Chart Type under the Design tab.

SmartArt

SmartArt is a dynamically generated, editable infographic. It is intended to speed the rendering and editing process. To add a SmartArt graphic, choose the Illustrations group in the Insert tab and select SmartArt. Enter your text by clicking [Text] in the Text pane, and then type your information. Text and visual elements remain editable.

Use Table 4-3 to select the best SmartArt graphic.

Table 4-3. Selecting SmartArt Graphics

SmartArt Graphic	Illustrates
List	A set of information
Process	A sequence
Cycle	A repeatable process

Table 4-3. Selecting SmartArt Graphics (cont.)

SmartArt Graphic	Illustrates
Hierarchy	Hierarchical structure
Relationship	Connections and correlations
Matrix	Groups of information
Pyramid	Hierarchical order
Picture	A set of pictures and information

I do not recommend SmartArt because it can be seen as unprofessional. Learners make quick judgments about your content based on what they see. If they think your materials were easily assembled or it is something they can do, the perceived value of your content is diminished. If you use SmartArt, consider these style tips:

1. Remove outlines. Outlines make your content look flat—like a cartoon.
2. Match the colors and styles to the rest of your presentation and learning materials.
3. Format your text (Figure 4-15).

Figure 4-15. Tips for Using SmartArt

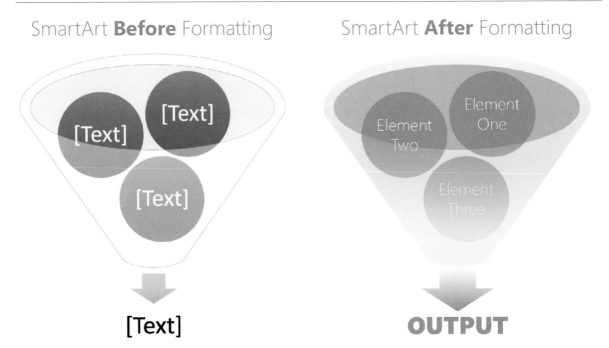

Animation

PowerPoint animation is a set of effects applied to objects so they will appear, move, highlight, or disappear in Slide Show mode. Before applying an animation, ensure it will help the learner better understand the slide. Never use an animation effect because it looks cool. Unfortunately, presenters enjoy playing with animations and will create effects that distract from their primary takeaway.

When applied properly and with thought, PowerPoint animations can tell stories and enhance explanations. I use animations to slowly introduce points on my slide. By revealing my points over time through animation, I am more likely to keep the focus on me because my audience will not be distracted reading the slide. Presentations that use animation as a storytelling device are more effective. Essentially, you're making mini movies that have a beginning, a middle, and an end. (As an example, see the DNA build animation in chapter 3.)

There are four types of animations in PowerPoint:

1. **Entrance:** Animates how your object enters the slide
2. **Emphasis:** Highlights, or draws attention to, an object
3. **Exit:** Animates how your object exits the slide
4. **Motion Path:** Animates your object along a defined path, such as lines, arcs, shapes, loops, and custom paths.

To apply an animation to an object, select your object, then pick your animation effect from the Animations tab. Use the Animation Pane to change the parameters of your animation. In the Animations Pane, you can modify these aspects:

- Change the order of an animation by selecting an animated object and clicking the up or down arrow.
- To delete an animation, select an animated object and either click the X or hit delete on your keyboard.
- To add another animation to the same object, select the animated object on the slide (not in the Animation Pane). Next, pick another animation from the Animation Tab.
- Effect Options give you the power to change the animated effect properties. These options are dependent upon the animation effect applied. You can also add a built-in or custom sound effect. (To add a sound, make sure it is an acceptable file format. Suitable sound file formats are dependent upon your operating system and PowerPoint version.)
- Change how your animation is activated, the duration, delay time, and repetition.
- Modify animated text effects by group, word, or letter.

With these options, you can make almost any animation you can imagine. Be flexible. Play with the effects to understand how animations and options affect your final product.

When you want to quickly apply the same animation to another object, select the object with the desired associated animation and click Animation Painter. Animation Painter has now collected the animation effect applied to that object. Next, click the object to which you want to apply the animation, and the effect will be transferred.

Tip: Double-click Animation Painter to retain the sampled animation and apply it to multiple objects. Click Escape to release the sampled animation.

Avoid pointless animations. Sometimes presenters think that their slides need something, so they make boxes fly in, have text swirl around, or include a spinning globe animated GIF. I call this "dancing bologna." It adds no value and distracts participants from valuable content. PowerPoint gives you the ability to animate anything—but just because you can doesn't mean you should. With a nod toward Stan Lee (who helped create Spider Man and other iconic comic characters), with great power comes great responsibility. Be judicious. Use animations wisely.

Transitions

A slide transition is an animated effect between two slides. Use a PowerPoint transition to improve flow and meaning. Never use it as a "gee whiz" effect; flashy transitions that deliver no value quickly lose their novelty and distract your audience from the content. If you apply slide transitions, be consistent. Do not use random transitions. You can use multiple transitions, but be sure it adds value and it's clear why you did it.

An effective use of a slide transition would be using Push to continue to the next slide. For example, if you were explaining an eight-step process and you have four steps on one slide and four on the next, a transition can seamlessly connect the two. By pushing the slide to the left (listed as From Right in PowerPoint) as you change slides, the perception is that you are revealing the second half of a long slide (Figure 4-16).

PowerPoint slide transitions are segmented into three groups:

- **Subtle:** These effects apply simple animations between two slides.
- **Exciting:** These are complex slide transition effects.
- **Dynamic Content:** These transition only the elements on your slides and not the static backgrounds. Dynamic content transitions use a subtle transition on any background elements that change. This transition effect can unify your story.

Figure 4-16. Push Transition

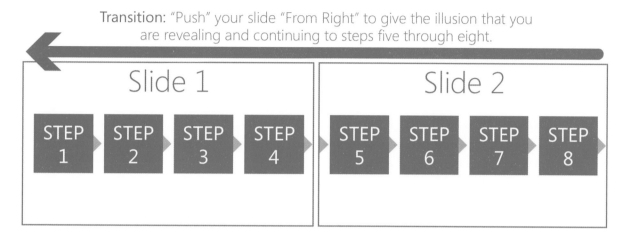

Transition: "Push" your slide "From Right" to give the illusion that you are revealing and continuing to steps five through eight.

To apply a slide transition effect, select one or more slides in the Slide Navigation pane. In the Transitions tab, select the transition you wish to apply. To modify your transition, select your slide with an existing transition effect and click Effect Options. The options available are dependent upon the applied transition effect. Change the duration and add a transition sound effect in the ribbon, if desired. To remove a transition effect, select your slide(s) and choose None.

The Morph transition automatically interpolates and animates a transition between like objects. It creates the appearance of movement. The Morph transition requires two slides with one or more objects in common. (PowerPoint has to know both items are connected.) To see how it works, duplicate a slide and move an object on the second slide. Apply the Morph transition to the second slide to see what Morph animates and how it moves your object. (You can also copy and paste objects from slide to slide and apply Morph to generate the same effect.)

Tip: The Apply To All ribbon command applies one slide transition to all slides in your presentation and over-writes any other transitions. Select None to remove the slide transition effects.

To give the illusion of zooming in on an object, create two versions of the same slide. On the second slide, increase the size of the object you want to zoom in on. Apply the Morph transition to the second slide. It will appear as if you are zooming into an element. If you go back to the previous slide, the Morph animation plays in reverse to give the illusion that you are zooming out.

To advance slides automatically, go to the Timing group in the ribbon and uncheck On Mouse Click. In the After field, add the duration you want a slide to appear onscreen. For example, if you choose 1:00, your slide will remain on the screen for one minute, and then automatically advance to the next slide in Slide Show mode.

Interactivity

There are three ways to create interactivity in PowerPoint:

1. **Hyperlink:** Adds a clickable link to a file, like a sound, movie, or presentation; an email address; a web address; or an object.
2. **Actions:** Adds a clickable link to a file, like a sound, movie, or presentation; an email address; a web address; or a built-in shape. Unlike a hyperlink, it can be activated by clicking on or hovering the cursor over the shape.
3. **Zoom:** Quickly adds interactive, nonlinear navigation using hyperlinked slides and sections.

Hyperlinks have two components: the linked file name or address and the displayed content (text, picture, or shape). To insert a hyperlink, select the object that you want to link. Right-click or control-click and select Hyperlink from the dialog list.

Existing File or Web Page links to local or online files. For example, you can link to another presentation or a website. Place in This Document links to objects in your current presentation. Create New Document opens a new PowerPoint document. E-mail Address inserts a linked email address. You can also add a screen tip to explain your link, which will appear when your learner's cursor hovers over the object.

"You can pair transitions and multiple animation effects."

—Tom Howell, Microsoft PowerPoint MVP

To edit, test, or remove a hyperlink, right-click or control-click and select Edit Hyperlink, Test Hyperlink, or Remove Hyperlink from the dialog list.

To insert an action button, click the Insert tab. Either click Action in the ribbon or, for predefined actions, click the Shapes command and select Action Buttons in the drop-down menu. Next, select the Mouse Click or Mouse Over tab. (Mouse Over actions are activated when the cursor is over the object and Mouse Click actions are activated when the cursor is over the object and is clicked.) Choose from no action (None), a hyperlink, run program, run macro (only available if your presentation contains a macro), or object action (only available for Object Linking and Embedding—or OLE—objects). Within the Action dialog box, you also have the option of playing a sound and/or highlighting when activated. You can apply different actions based on whether your action shape is hovered over or clicked.

Action buttons can be formatted like any other object using Format Shape. For example, you can apply brand standards, or make them invisible. To test your action button, go to Slide Show view and activate your button. To edit your action button, select your

button and click Actions in the Insert tab. To delete your action button, select the button and click delete on your keyboard.

Zoom is an interactive effect that contextualizes your content. It orients your learner back to a previous slide or landing page through the zoom transition effect. To use Zoom, go to the Insert tab and choose from three options: Summary Zoom, Slide Zoom, and Section Zoom.

Summary Zoom automatically creates a central landing slide (Summary Zoom slide) for sections of your choosing within your presentation. In essence, it makes a table of contents with clickable pictures. This function places thumbnail images of each section or slide you select on a Summary Zoom slide. To apply Summary Zoom, go to the Insert tab and click on Zoom. Click Summary Zoom to activate the dialog box. The default setting starts at each section, if any, or you can select specific slides and the slides or sections to include. These will become the first slides of your Summary Zoom sections. If you already have sections in your presentation, the first slide of each section will be shown by default. Deselect sections you don't want included. Click Keep Unused Sections in Your Presentation when you want PowerPoint to retain the sections you didn't include in your Summary Zoom. At the end of each section, you'll automatically return to the Summary Zoom slide. To add or remove sections, go to the Format tab and select Edit Summary. Change the sections as needed and click Update (Figure 4-17).

Don't see the Format tab? Tabs are contextual; they only appear when you can use them.

Slide Zoom links to slides you choose in your presentation. It's mainly used to create a smooth transition or animated effect, and does not automatically return to the summary slide. To apply Slide Zoom, go to the Insert tab and click Zoom. Choose Slide Zoom to activate the dialog box. Select the slides to include and click Insert. Your Slide Zoom is created.

Section Zoom links to existing sections you choose in your presentation. It functions just like Summary Zoom but only works with sections. (If you have not created sections, this option will not be available.) To apply Section Zoom, go to the Insert tab and click on Zoom. Click Section Zoom to activate the dialog box. Select the sections to include and click Insert. Your Section Zoom is created (Figure 4-18).

Figure 4-17. Using Summary Zoom

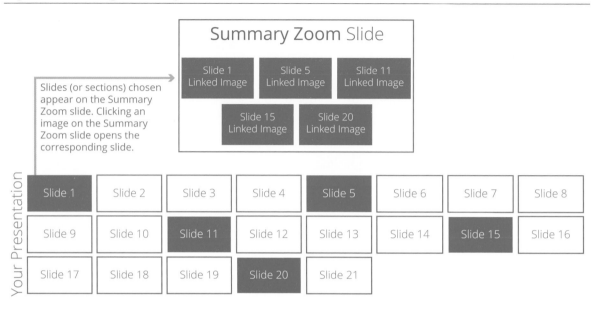

Figure 4-18. Creating Section Zoom

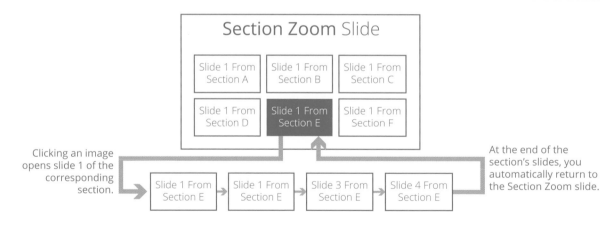

Clicking Return to Zoom under Zoom Options ensures you return to the main Zoom slide. To do so, click on a Zoom-generated thumbnail and select the Format tab, and you'll have a host of options, which includes Return to Zoom. (Summary Zoom or a Section Zoom returns automatically.) If you don't want to use the zoom transition, or if you want to change the duration of the transition, go to Zoom Options and uncheck Zoom Transition or change the duration (shown in seconds). To turn off (and on) the background of a Zoom-generated thumbnail, right-click the thumbnail and select Zoom Background. This feature only works if the background of the thumbnail is the template or slide's background. It does not work if you manually add an image behind your content.

Insert Pictures, Video, and Audio

To add external elements to your PowerPoint slides, go to the Insert tab and select Pictures, Video, or Audio. All images, video, and sound must be a file type recognized by your version of PowerPoint in order to import them. Adding pictures is as simple as navigating to the image you want to add and selecting it. Inserting Video allows you to link locally (for example, on your computer) or to an online video. Linking to an online video requires an Internet connection and enough bandwidth for smooth playback. Resize and reposition your images and videos as needed. You can add existing sound files or a sound you record using a digital recording dialog box for audio additions. To play an inserted audio file, go to the Slide Show mode and click on the audio image.

Pictures, video, and audio are embedded into your PowerPoint document by default. This means that the file size of your document will increase by the size of each inserted element. (Files can be linked to reduce file size, but the linked files must always travel with your PowerPoint file.)

High-quality, professional photographs, images, videos, and sounds signal high-quality content. Using unprofessional, low-quality content of any kind tells your audience that your content may not be worth their time.

Editing Pictures, Video, and Audio

PowerPoint supplies some editing abilities for imported elements. To edit images, select your photograph and go to the Format tab. From there you can crop, recolor, reposition, resize, remove unwanted image elements (for example, the background), and apply effects. The tool I use most is Crop. Adding "fancy" effects can lower the perceived quality of your presentations. Use the effects in the Format tab to either increase the quality of your image or ensure the style is consistent with your other images.

To edit video, click on your video and select the Format tab or the Playback tab. In the Format tab, focus on Poster Frame (that is, the default image that appears before the video is played) and Crop. For video playback, use the following tools:

- **Add and Remove Bookmark:** Insert a bookmark to trigger animations at a specific point (Animation/Trigger/On Bookmark) or to jump to a specific location in a video.

- **Trim Video:** Allows you to cut away unwanted video portions.
- **Fade In and Out:** Fades video in or out based on the duration (in seconds) entered.
- **Volume:** Sets the default playback volume.
- **Start Options:** Choose between When Clicked On to play your video when clicked or Automatically to start playback when the slide appears.

Editing audio offers similar editing options as video:

- **Add and Remove Bookmark:** Insert a bookmark to trigger animations at a specific point (Animation/Trigger/On Bookmark) or to jump to a specific location in an audio clip.
- **Trim Audio:** Allows you to cut away unwanted audio portions.
- **Fade In and Out:** Fades audio in or out based on the duration (in seconds) entered.
- **Volume:** Sets the default playback volume.
- **Start Options:** Choose between When Clicked On to play your audio when clicked or Play to start playback when the slide appears.
- **Loop When Played Back:** Select when looping (repeating) ambient music or sound effects.

Resolution

Raster and vector are the only two visual formats used in PowerPoint. For our purposes, raster images are photographs. They consist of hundreds to millions of tiny dots, or pixels. The greater the dot density (the number of dots per inch—dpi), the higher the quality of the image and the larger the file size. Raster images are resolution dependent. This means that you need to know the final dimensions and media on which your PowerPoint content will be shared to ensure sufficient quality. For printing, your raster images should be 200 dpi or better. (Based on my experience, 300 dpi offers the highest-quality printing, but 200 dpi is an acceptable quality and results lower file sizes). The larger you scale a raster image, the more resolution it loses. Most images found on the web are screen resolution (72-96 dpi), which means they look good onscreen but do not print well. Lower-resolution images look fuzzy, distorted, jagged, and unprofessional (Figure 4-19).

> "It's becoming a video-first culture. Why animate and make videos in PowerPoint? Because it's flexible, faster, and less expensive than the alternative."
>
> —Tom Howell,
> Microsoft PowerPoint MVP

Figure 4-19. Examples of Image Resolution

When you save a slide as an image (for example, a JPG, TIFF, PNG, GIF, or BMP), it becomes a raster image, and the default resolution is 72 or 96 dpi. To export files as print resolution raster files, use Image Export (www.pptools.com) for Windows. On a Mac, increase the dimensions of your slides and scale them down in a package like Microsoft Word or Adobe Photoshop to increase their dpi. Use a website like Auction Repair (http://auctionrepair.com/pixels.html) to calculate the final resolution of an exported raster image to ensure it is print quality.

Vector images are resolution independent: You can scale them to any size, and they will retain a high image quality. They print well and have lower file sizes. They are created in software programs like PowerPoint, which use math to determine points, lines, curves, color, and other visual properties. The most common vector elements in PowerPoint are fonts, shapes, charts, and SmartArt (Figure 4-20). Popular vector file formats include AI, EMF, EPS, SVG, and WMF. Saving your file as a PDF maintains vector and raster formats for all elements in your PowerPoint document.

> Tip: All web imagery is protected by copyright law, and is usually at a resolution and dimension unsuitable for print. Some sites grant the rights to reuse their imagery dependent upon purpose. Always check the rights of use to avoid fines or litigation.

Figure 4-20. Vector and Raster Comparisons

Vector

Raster

Example: Clip Art

Example: Photograph

Resolution Independent

Resolution Dependent
(file size varies greatly when creating)

Easily Manipulated

Time Consuming to Manipulate

Visually More Rudimentary

More Visually Appealing
(if done improperly, less communicative)

Exporting and Sharing (File Types)

PowerPoint can be saved and shared as multiple file formats. Access your options under the Save As command. The following is a list of the most popular formats and their applications:

- **PowerPoint Presentation (PPTX):** Creates an editable PowerPoint file. Compatible with the current versions of the software. Use this file type to share and give others the ability to edit your content. Anyone with PowerPoint 2007 or newer can open and edit this file type.
- **PowerPoint Macro-Enabled Presentation (PPTX):** Same as the previous format, but you can include macros. A macro is a set of commands to automate a task.
- **PDF (PDF):** Saves your presentation as a printable file. Hyperlinks and actions work, but animations and slide transitions don't. The file is no longer editable in PowerPoint. However, some modifications can be made using Adobe Acrobat or another software program that reads PDF.
- **PowerPoint Template (POTX):** A file used as a "blueprint" with defined layouts, backgrounds, fonts, styles, and formatting. Anyone with PowerPoint 2007 or newer can open and edit this file type. Use this format to maintain layout and styles across many PPTX files.

- **PowerPoint Macro-Enabled Template (POTX):** A file used as a "blueprint" with defined layouts, backgrounds, fonts, styles, and formatting, including macros.
- **Office Theme (THMX):** Saves your colors, fonts, and effects as a theme that can be imported into another PowerPoint file. You can apply your THMX file to other presentations by selecting the Design tab and choosing Browse for Themes in the Theme section of the ribbon. Navigate to your THMX file and select it, and your theme will be automatically applied.
- **PowerPoint Show (PPSX):** Automatically opens your presentation in Slide Show mode. To open a PPSX file, you need Microsoft's free PowerPoint viewer or PowerPoint 2007 or newer.
- **PowerPoint Macro-Enabled Show (PPSX):** Same as the previous format, but you can include Macros.
- **MPEG-4 Video (MP4):** Saves your slide deck as a video. An MP4 is also known as an MPEG-4 file. Slides advance approximately every five seconds unless you change the timing within a PowerPoint transition duration. (Animations play as if you were advancing the slides by clicking.) To view an MP4, you need a video player like Windows Media Player or QuickTime. The video of your presentation is only editable in video-editing software. Sound, transition, and timing are editable, but slide content is not.
- **Windows Media Video (WMV):** Saves your slide deck as a video. Slides advance approximately every five seconds unless you change the timing within a PowerPoint transition duration. (Animations play as if you were advancing the slides by clicking.) To view a WMV, you need a video player like Windows Media Player, VLC, DivX Player, KMPlayer, or MPlayer. Sound, transition, and timing are editable using video-editing software. Your slide content is no longer editable.
- **JPEG File Interchange Format (JPG or JPEG):** Saves slides as raster images. You can export one or more slides. Once exported as images, the JPEG files are no longer editable without image editing software.

When sharing your editable presentation, you can embed fonts in the Windows operating system (OS), but not in a Mac OS. To embed fonts, select Options under the File tab and then select Save. Click Embed Fonts and choose the best option for your needs.

Grouping

Use PowerPoint's Group function to organize, animate, or scale multiple objects. To use Group and Ungroup, select multiple objects (hold your Shift key to select many shapes). In the Home tab, select Arrange and then Group or Ungroup depending upon your needs. There can be nested groups—groups within groups—to better organize and work with your slide content.

"To get a higher-quality company logo (not vector), find a PDF of the company logo embedded and open it. Zoom to the logo and take a screen grab. Insert your screen grab in PowerPoint and modify as desired. Make sure you have permission if your presentation isn't protected under fair use laws."

—Steve Rindsberg, Microsoft PowerPoint MVP

Recording

First, create a script so you know what you want to say. For some versions of PowerPoint, the Recording tab is not a default option. To access the Recording tab, go to the File tab and click Options. Then select the Customize Ribbon link. Next, under Customize Ribbon in the right-hand box, check the Recording box and click OK.

When you are ready to record, select the Recording tab (Slide Show tab for Mac) and click Record Slide Show. In older versions of PowerPoint, you can also click the Record Slide Show down arrow to access other options such as Record from Beginning and Record from Current Slide. Select Slide and Animation Timings (use Timings on Mac) if you want to use preset duration settings. Select the Narrations, Ink, and Laser Pointer option (use Timings, Show Media Controls on Mac) if you want to record a voice-over and your cursor movement and screen actions. To record sound, you need a microphone, which is usually built into the computer or can be acquired.

If recording does not start immediately, begin recording by clicking the red Record symbol. At any time, you can click the pause button and then choose Resume Recording when you are ready to continue. Your presentation recording is automatically saved after you are finished. You can find your timings beneath each slide in the Slide Sorter view, and your voice-overs at the bottom right of your slides in the Normal view.

To clear audio and timing, click on the Record Slide Show down arrow and choose from four options:

1. Delete the timings on the currently selected slide.
2. Delete the timings on all slides at once.
3. Delete the narration on the currently selected slide.

4. Delete the narrations on all slides at once.

Select the option that meets your needs. You can then either manually set your slide durations or rerecord specific slides using Record Current Slide. (You can also manually delete the sound symbol from your slides and change the timings under Transitions/Duration.)

If you want to share your recording, under the Recording tab, click Export to Video. You can

> "Look around you. Take pictures. Keep a source file or idea board of new color palettes, textures, typography treatments, graphic styles, and so on. Use a digital notebook to keep your online finds. Don't be a copycat, though! Transform and combine ideas from your inspiration sources to create your own unique designs."
>
> —Julie Terberg, Microsoft PowerPoint MVP

choose the quality of your recording as well as other timing options. (Higher-quality video increases file size and fidelity.) Click Create Video to save your video for sharing. It can take several minutes to several hours to complete the process, depending upon the size and length of your presentation. The larger the presentation, the longer it will take to save. A progress bar appears at the bottom of you PowerPoint interface so you can monitor the process.

Summary

Keep your visuals simple and always have a purpose for every aesthetic decision. Do not use unclear, complex, or low-quality graphics, video, or sound. Label elements directly and avoid legends on slides. Buy a graphic or hire a designer for those images that are beyond your skill level.

With practice, using what you learn in this book, you can make your own professional PowerPoint content. Give yourself a project and seek more knowledge as new needs arise. Every time you use what you have learned, you are one step closer to being a PowerPoint guru. Practice is key.

Inspiration is everywhere you look. Study webpages, books, magazines, television, and ads. Find items that inspire you and save them for future reference.

Use this checklist when creating graphics in PowerPoint:

☐ **Learn key PowerPoint features.**
☐ **Practice and give yourself projects.**
☐ **Buy or build what you need.**
☐ **Make an inspiration file.**

5

Render: Design Principles for Professional Slides

PowerPoint is structured to take advantage of the design principles I share in this book. The software encourages the application of these best practices. Applying what you learn in this section increases the professionalism of your presentation and improves the odds that your content will be understood and remembered.

There are seven elements of art (line, shape, form, space, texture, color, and value) and seven principles of design (pattern, balance, emphasis, contrast, unity, rhythm, and movement). Design principles explain how an artist uses the science of aesthetics to control the viewer's experience. For the purposes of learning PowerPoint, here are my nine design principles. They're a hybrid of the traditional design elements and principles and optimized for PowerPoint:

1. color
2. balance and symmetry
3. unity and harmony
4. shapes and lines
5. visual noise
6. hierarchy
7. layout
8. text
9. visuals.

Each plays a major role in the quality and professionalism of your presentation and Power-Point learning materials. I cannot stress this enough: These nine design principles should be the foundation of every aesthetic decision you make.

When rendering slides, all aesthetic decisions should have a reason behind them. To be effective, design choices must clearly support your message. If you ask, "Why are we using this graphic or design element?" and the answer is, "Because it looks cool," then delete it and find another enhancement strategy.

For example, when I make corporate templates, I reinforce the brand consciously and unconsciously by using color, fonts, and style, and by using parts of the logo in the design elements. I have found that repeated exposure to a consistent brand identity builds trust.

Color

Color is the first thing your participants see when they look at your content. According to Lynell Burmark, author of *Visual Literacy: Learn to See, See to Learn* (2002), using color enhances learning and increases retention by more than 75 percent. It is one of the most effective ways to influence mood. Colors evoke specific emotional responses, and the meaning of a color is culturally and subject dependent.

Here is a list of colors and their corresponding emotional, unconscious reactions (specific to many Western cultures):

- Red = empowering, bold (Like all colors, red affects us emotionally, eliciting a physical reaction. For example, seeing the color red decreases response time; Martinez-Conde and Macknik 2014; University of Rochester 2011.)
- Orange = warmth, happiness
- Yellow = happiness, energy (excellent for highlighting)
- Green = balance, refreshing (usually makes a good secondary color)
- Blue = relaxing, cool (usually the safest and most appealing color to use for business graphic color schemes)
- Violet = comforting
- White = pure, associated with cleanliness
- Black = authoritative, shows discipline.

In some regions of the world, red evokes very different emotions and concepts. For example, in China, red is the color of happiness and prosperity. In India and Pakistan, brides wear red. In South Africa, it is the color of mourning. Before choosing a color, know your learner (see the Discover phase). Research how your audience will interpret your aesthetic choices. Learn as much as you can about your target audience prior to choosing your color palette to ensure the clearest communication and predictable emotional responses.

Use the acronym ROY G. BV to remember the color positions on the wheel (Figure 5-1).

Figure 5-1. The Color Wheel

Color consists of three variables:

- **Hue:** where the color appears on the color wheel
- **Saturation:** the intensity or vibrancy of the color
- **Value:** the lightness or darkness of the color.

Colors are often associated with temperature:

- **Warm colors:** red, orange, yellow
- **Cool colors:** green, blue, purple (violet).

There are also two frequently referenced "groupings" of colors:

- **Analogous:** colors that appear next to one another on the color wheel, like blue, green, and yellow
- **Complementary:** colors that are across from one another on the color wheel, like red and green.

Analogous colors are often the better choice when developing your color palette because complementary colors vibrate when next to one another.

In Figure 5-2, color affects the appeal of each pie. Both images of the pie evoke different unconscious responses.

Figure 5-2. Which Pie Would You Rather Eat?

Green and gray are not typically associated with tasty foods. When many foods go bad, the color changes to a hue similar to the one shown on the right. For these reasons, warm colors, such as red, can be considered more appetizing.

Use color to explain and steer your audience's unconscious responses. Make it easy for them to "see" what you are saying. Red in many Western cultures can be associated with danger. In Figure 5-3, red is associated with a negative concept (risk), whereas green is associated with a positive concept (safety).

Figure 5-3. A Risk Matrix According to Color

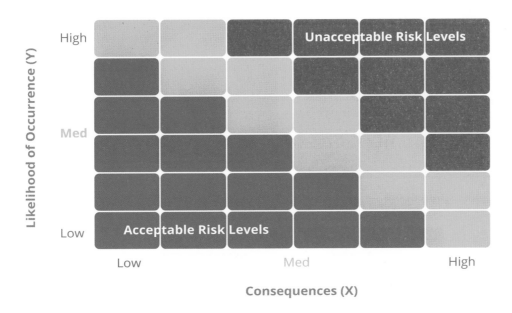

When choosing colors for your PowerPoint materials, consider your goals. For example, if you want to brand your organization, use your organization's colors. If you want to build trust, use your learners' corporate colors, because familiarity breeds trust. If you want to play it safe with universally appealing colors, use blues and greens. Blue, and to a lesser extent green, are considered the most appealing colors in most cultures.

- Color can improve readership by 40 percent.
- Color improves learning from 55 to 78 percent.
- Color improves comprehension up to 73 percent.
  —Johnson (1992)

Be flexible when working with color. Color fidelity is unlikely when presenting your PowerPoint content; every monitor, projector, and printer will display colors differently. The lighting in a room changes what we see. Women usually see more colors than men. Color is also relative to surrounding or neighboring colors.

Be consistent; select one color palette or set of RGB values (or another color selection scale) and stay with them. A harmonious, uniform, limited color palette demonstrates professionalism. When needed, use online color-picking tools to select a professional palette (Figure 5-4).

Figure 5-4. Examples of Professional Color Palettes

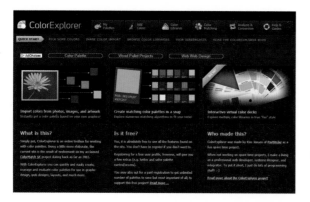

colorexplorer.com

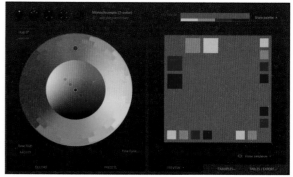

paletton.com

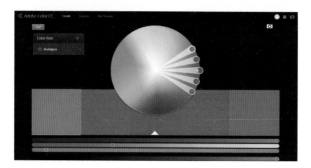

color.adobe.com

Balance and Symmetry

Balance and symmetry are two design elements that affect professionalism. Balanced slides and graphics communicate stability and encourage a positive state of mind. Unbalanced content creates a feeling of uneasiness. Aesthetic balance is achieved when your slide's left and right sides (and, to a lesser extent, top and bottom) visually "weigh" similar amounts, giving a sense of equilibrium.

Unbalanced slides and graphics look as if they will tip to one side because the elements are positioned unevenly (Figure 5-5). True symmetry is achieved if half your slide or graphic mirrors the other half (Figure 5-6). Aesthetically symmetrical slides and graphics give a sense of order and stability, but they can be seen as an uninspiring, boring design.

Figure 5-5. Achieving Balanced Slide Content

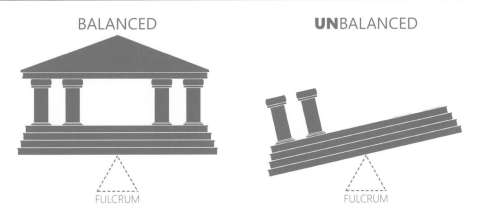

Figure 5-6. Creating Symmetrical Slides

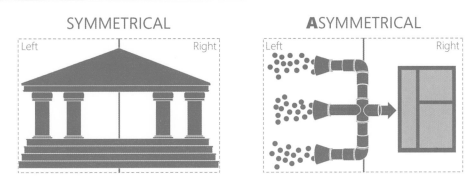

Symmetry is not required to achieve balance (see the asymmetrical image in Figure 5-6). Asymmetrical balance is more frequently used in professional design. Your learners are less affected by visual balance, but unbalance has a more pronounced, negative impact. It is almost impossible to achieve perfect visual balance, so don't be overly concerned with it. Get as close as you can, and be aware of egregious balance issues. If your goal is to create interesting, dynamic slides or graphics, use asymmetrical balance. It is considered more professional.

Use your knowledge of the effect balance and symmetry have on your audience when making design and layout decisions. Never allow balance and symmetry to be the main tool when motivating your learners to pay attention.

Unity and Harmony

Harmonious slides denote professionalism. Harmony is the result of aesthetic accord, and it evokes feelings of trust. The best way to achieve harmony is to create and follow a template. Your template defines the look, feel, and voice of your PowerPoint content. To create a template, first define every element you can imagine, such as:

- dimensions
- key terms
- acronyms
- special characters
- fonts
- capitalization
- punctuation
- writing style
- graphic styles
- layout

- color palette
- box styles
- line styles
- arrow styles
- photo styles
- animation styles
- video treatment
- icons and symbols
- callouts
- logos.

Figure 5-7 is an example of a PowerPoint template. Use it as a guideline to create your own. Add or remove frequently needed content and elements according to your needs.

Figure 5-7. PowerPoint Template

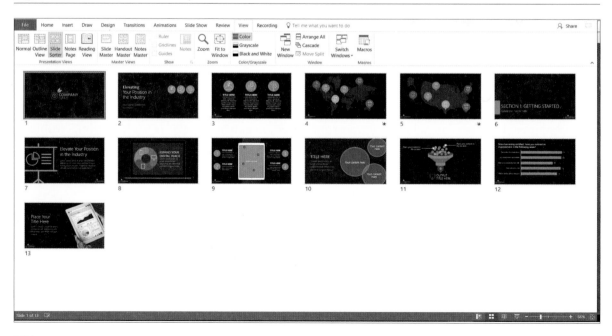

Factors that influence unity and harmony are proximity, similarity, repetition, rhythm, and continuation. Proximity is the distance between elements. Objects can feel crowded if they're too close together, or they can feel open by adding space (that is, white space). Similarity refers to the consistency of all elements. Uniformity without being boring is your goal. Use repetition—defined, reused elements—throughout your presentation as breadcrumbs or connectors. Rhythm establishes a pattern using cadence. Continuation extends a pattern into space and time (Figure 5-8).

Figure 5-8. Factors Influencing Harmony

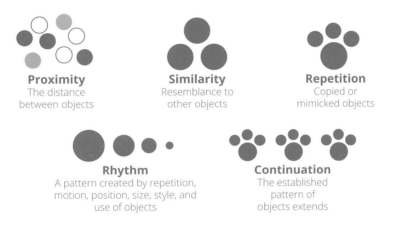

If you want to grab your audience's attention, use safe surprises, such as a pattern interrupt. Occasionally include something that is inconsistent with your established template, an element that breaks the rules of harmony. It could be a new way to present content, a style change, a switch in your narrative voice, or an incongruent sound. For example, your template's background is black with simple designs and clean text. On one slide, use a white background with busy content. Your learners will pay more attention to that which is different. Be sure to use this tactic when appropriate—and infrequently. Overuse or misuse negatively affects learning and lessens the impact of this effect.

> "You don't need to fill the entire slide with content. White space is an important component of good design. Surround important design elements with plenty of white space to make them stand out."
>
> —Julie Terberg,
> Microsoft PowerPoint MVP

Shapes and Lines

Shapes and lines also affect the mood of your learners and your perceived professionalism. Diagonal shapes and lines are seen as dynamic and energetic, but used incorrectly, they can make the learner anxious or agitated. Too many diagonals, for example, result in a slide that lacks order and feels messy, and the associated content is usually difficult to follow. Horizontal and vertical shapes and lines convey a sense of stability. Content feels organized and ordered, but can seem predictable and boring. Curved shapes and lines are comforting and relaxing and can help calm your audience (Figure 5-9).

Figure 5-9. Using Different Shapes and Lines

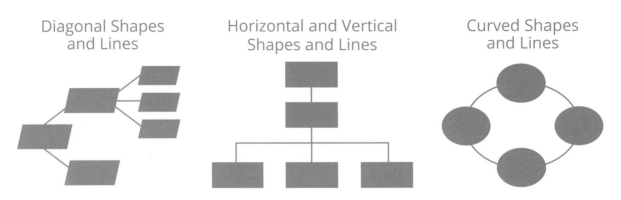

Choose shapes and lines that support the message and feelings you wish to convey and elicit. Some shapes have predefined meanings based on subject matter and culture. For example, in process diagrams, shapes have meaning to those who know the visual vocabulary. Do your homework before choosing identifiable shapes, such as those in a technical process diagram (Figure 5-10).

Figure 5-10. Common Process Diagram Symbols

There are many more process diagram symbols. In my experience, the average person does not know their meanings. Be sure your audience understands each symbol before using it.

Visual Noise

Using too many graphical elements or complex textures causes visual noise. Your content will be considered "too busy." Visual noise often looks unprofessional, so keep your content as simple as possible. Figure 5-11 is a PowerPoint infographic template that shows the difference that background noise (in this case a texture) can make regarding professionalism and legibility.

Figure 5-11. Understanding Visual Noise

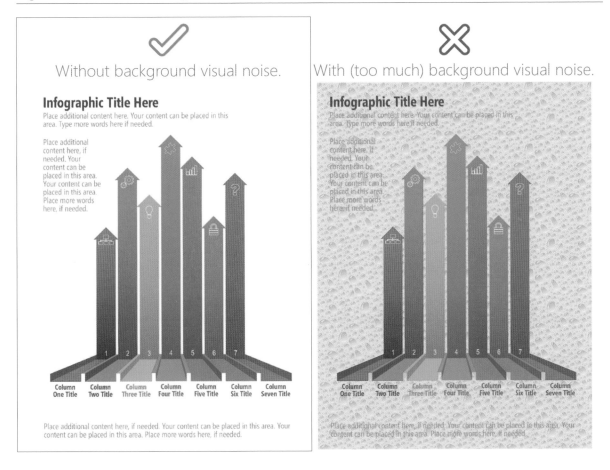

You can use visual noise to your advantage, though, if your intent is to sway your target audience's opinion from something unwanted or unfavorable. To use this technique, create a graphic depicting two elements: old and new or before and after. Show the old element with lots of visual

> "Less is more. When your audience is reading your slide, they're not listening to you."
>
> —Echo Swinford,
> Microsoft PowerPoint MVP

noise. Show the new element clutter-free, organized, and easy to read. The learner will be drawn to the cleaner, more digestible portion of your graphic.

However, don't make the unwanted or unfavorable portion of your graphic overtly cluttered, or your intent will be too obvious. Your audience may feel manipulated.

Hierarchy

Your content needs to lead your audience through your story. Some content is more important and should be dominant. But for something to be seen as having greater visual significance, other things must recede; there must be hierarchy. Dominance is established by emphasizing one element and de-emphasizing others.

Aesthetic hierarchy and highlighting are achieved through the relativity of surrounding elements. Too many visually dominant graphic elements diminish the effect and often result in an unsuccessful slide or graphic. Use relative color, shade, positioning, size, or complexity to focus your learners' attention (Figure 5-12).

Figure 5-12. Principles of Aesthetic Hierarchy

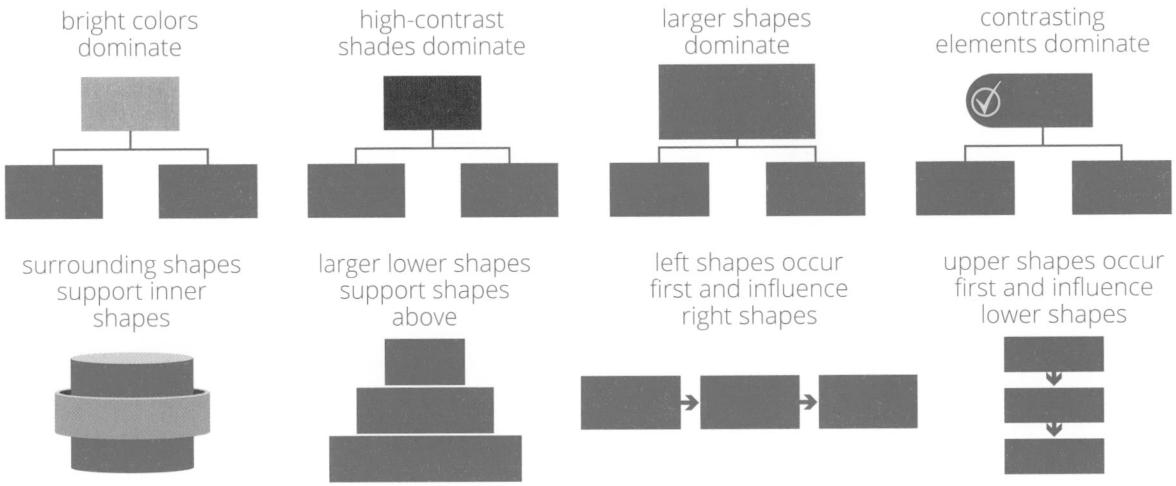

bright colors dominate

high-contrast shades dominate

larger shapes dominate

contrasting elements dominate

surrounding shapes support inner shapes

larger lower shapes support shapes above

left shapes occur first and influence right shapes

upper shapes occur first and influence lower shapes

Hierarchy applies to your layout, graphics, story, and architecture. For example, your message might be your title. Hierarchically, the title is the primary element, and the other content supports or proves your takeaway.

Layout (Grid)

Whether you are developing slides or handouts, position all PowerPoint elements using an invisible grid to support balance, consistency, rhythm, and harmony. A grid is an invisible skeleton for your slides and learning materials. It is the glue that binds all elements on your slides and pages. Not following a grid usually results in a disordered, unprofessional appearance. One the Home tab, under Arrange, use Align and Distribute Objects to adhere to your invisible grid (Figure 5-13).

"I encourage all those who create PowerPoint slides to work on a grid. If your slide template is created properly, the . . . placeholders will have been set up on a grid, so you should adhere to the spacing [and] layout guidelines established in those layouts. At the bare minimum, respect the margins. Nothing screams rookie more than a slide with inconsistent margins and content crammed to the slide edges."

—Sandra Johnson,
Microsoft PowerPoint MVP

Figure 5-13. Using a Grid to Order Slides

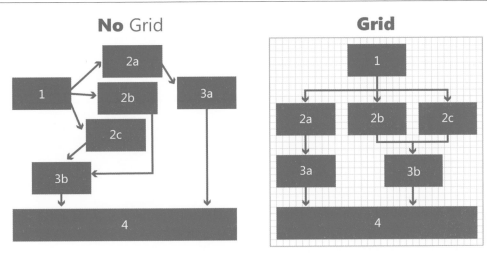

Text

Text can be used not only to communicate written content, but also as a design element. In Figure 5-14, the number 5 plays a dominant role in the layout and design.

Figure 5-14. Using Text in Design

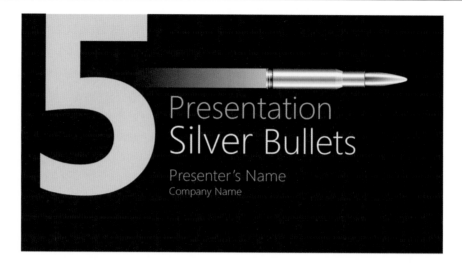

In Figure 5-15, words are the focal points in the slide. The photograph, circles, styles, positioning, and text size control where participants look and what message they receive from the slide. The imagery is supportive. This approach adds visual interest, which reinforces your content.

Figure 5-15. Making Words the Focus

There are two types of fonts: serif and sans serif. The difference lies in whether the font has a feature called a serif at the ends of each letter (Figure 5-16). Serif fonts work well for dense, text-heavy materials such as books or news articles, because many industry experts believe they are easier to read. Sans serif fonts stand out as headings and callouts, and are used widely on websites and for electronic devices. Designers debate the readability of each style and how they should be used. Sans serif fonts connote a modern aesthetic, whereas traditional-styled serif fonts can be viewed as vintage or corporate. Ultimately, you should choose a style that supports how you want to be seen and aligns with your content, business, or audience.

Figure 5-16. Serif and Sans Serif Fonts

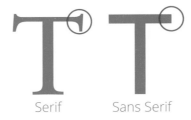

Serif   Sans Serif

For most situations, I recommend sans serif font like Helvetica, Futura, or Universe. Avoid font substitution issues by either embedding your fonts or using a ubiquitous font—that is, one installed on almost every computer in the world. Font substitution occurs if your font is not embedded or installed on the end user's machine. The software will then replace your font with another, and the visual integrity of your presentation may be lost.

> "To remove all formatting in a PowerPoint text box, select your text and click Control + Spacebar."
>
> —John Wilson, Microsoft PowerPoint MVP

The safest fonts for PowerPoint presentations are Times New Roman and Arial. However, you'll find that these other fonts are also installed on most Windows and Mac computers:

- Arial Black
- Book Antiqua
- Bookman Old Style
- Bradley Hand ITC
- Calibri
- Cambria
- Century
- Century Gothic
- Comic Sans
- Corbel
- Courier New
- Franklin Gothic
- Freestyle Script
- Garamond
- Georgia

- Impact
- Lucida Console
- Lucida Handwriting
- Mistral
- Monotype Corsiva
- Palatino Linotype
- Papyrus
- Tahoma
- Trebuchet MS
- Verdana
- Wingdings.

Select a legible font and limit how many fonts you use. Too many fonts in one PowerPoint document will likely look amateurish. (Experienced designers may use multiple fonts. When done right, the look can be very distinct. When done wrong, the result is a PowerPoint document that can look unprofessional.)

Tip: I recommend fonts no smaller than 14 point for projected PowerPoint presentations and no smaller than 8 point for printed PowerPoint learning materials.

Font styles range from simple to complex, new or vintage, and your font choice influences how your PowerPoint material is perceived. For example, if you want to be seen as safe and traditional, select a traditional font like Times New Roman. Figure 5-17 demonstrates how each font elicits a different perception.

Figure 5-17. Fonts Create Different Perceptions

Brush Script   Chalkboard

Cooper   Curlz

Giddyup   Goudy Old Style

Helvetica   HERCULANUM

Impact   Lucida Blackletter

MESQUITE   ROSEWOOD

STENCIL   Zapfino

What did Rosewood remind you of? How did you feel? Pick the font that best supports how you want your PowerPoint to be viewed. If your topic is serious, do not use a whimsical font like Curlz. Instead, try a visually clean font, such as Helvetica. Like any visual element, fonts have pre-existing, subject-specific, and culturally dependent associations. Choose your fonts wisely.

Use different fonts to support your takeaway and influence how your content is perceived, as shown in Figure 5-18.

Figure 5-18. Using Fonts

Design uses a blurry font bleeding off the edges to reinforce the title's message.

Visuals

When rendering graphics in PowerPoint, keep it simple, break elements down into basic shapes, and get inspired. Simplicity improves understanding. Disassembling your visuals into basic shapes makes it easier to understand how to build graphics with Merge (or Combine) Shapes. (See the Merge Shapes section in chapter 4 for step-by-step instructions.)

I use visuals and visual elements to influence emotions and improve education. Aesthetic choices change audience perception and elicit specific emotions. Perception and emotion affect learning. Using the design principles in this section can help

> "Simplicity and clarity are two of the most important principles to keep in mind when designing presentations. Less clutter and less content can help your audience focus on the message you're trying to convey."
>
> —Julie Terberg,
> Microsoft PowerPoint MVP

you steer what your participants think about your content. Through visuals, you can improve the perceived professionalism of your presentation. As discussed previously, color alone prompts certain feelings in your learners. The correct visual choices help engage your audience consciously and unconsciously.

Educational graphics clarify and explain your content. I use four overlapping graphic groups in my PowerPoint presentations: infographics, symbols, quantitative charts, and photographs.

Infographics

Informational graphics, or infographics, use any means (and graphic type) necessary to improve understanding. Infographics can include symbols, quantitative charts, and photographs; most use visual metaphors to communicate. For example, to explain transition, consider a bridge infographic. One side is the current situation, and the opposite side is the goal state (Figure 5-19).

Figure 5-19. An Infographic Shows Transition With a Bridge Metaphor

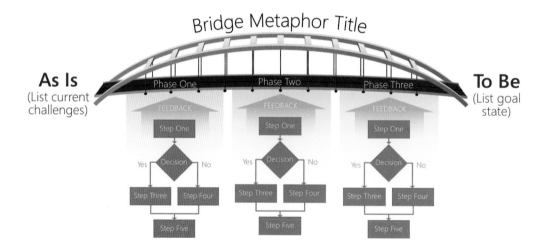

Using a visual metaphor tells a brief story and contextualizes your content. In this case, the bridge metaphor intuitively communicates stability, connection, span, and other descriptors your learners associate with this image. A visual metaphor supports your messages consciously and unconsciously. (Use the graphic types in appendix A to select the best graphic to meet your needs.)

As with colors and fonts, the style of your infographic sends a message to your learner. For example, a layout with a simplified, clean aesthetic tells your audience that the content is modern and, perhaps, innovative. A traditional aesthetic communicates that your content is established and trusted. Style is another visual queue that engages your learner unconsciously. The styles of the three infographics in Figure 5-20 convey different messages. For example, the left-most infographic uses large text, a relatively fun font, saturated colors, and a cartoon-like style. These choices make the content more approachable and appealing to certain audiences. Compare that with the center infographic, which uses a traditional font and icons with subdued, mostly monochromatic colors. As a result, it is perceived to be more academic. The third design's aesthetic choices sends yet another message to its target audience. Style plays a critical role in how you and your content are perceived.

Figure 5-20. Infographics Conveying Different Messages

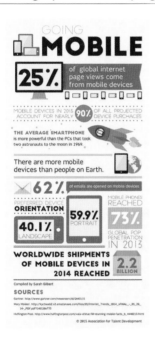 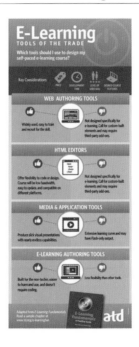 

To add your content, chunk the information and reassemble it to tell a story. It's the same process you use when storyboarding to conceptualize and render your PowerPoint graphics.

Symbols

Symbols are representational graphic elements that have a learned meaning, such as accepted marks that represent an action, concept, or entity (Figure 5-21). You can use any image as long as it is logically relevant to your subject matter. Use insight into your target audience to establish relevancy.

Figure 5-21. Using Relevant Symbols

Ionizing Radiation   Medical, Pharmacy, Doctor   Medical, Medicine   Idea, Innovation   No   Recycle

Symbols can connect your motivators (highest-level messages) to tactical activities (features of your content). For example, the symbols in Figure 5-22 show how each activity delivers specific benefits.

Figure 5-22. Using Symbols to Connect the Dots

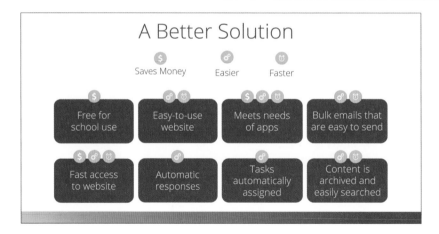

Quantitative Charts

Quantitative charts present data in a way that is easy to understand and act upon. There are two needs when presenting data: analysis or explanation. If you present data without explanation, your learner will need to analyze the information. For example, Figure 5-23 is a collection of data, with no perceived guidance or goal for the audience.

Figure 5-23. A Presentation of Data Without Analysis

```
2 5 0 3 8 1 3 5 6 9 2 9 9 4
3 9 3 2 7 4 1 2 4 9 0 6 4 0
4 0 4 8 2 0 1 0 4 8 6 7 2 3
2 0 5 6 5 9 1 2 0 2 1 4 6 5
8 6 3 7 6 3 6 2 2 8 3 5 0 6
9 0 4 5 6 6 9 2 8 1 0 5 4 9
3 9 4 6 1 9 2 0 2 0 4 5 7 5
1 0 4 5 6 9 0 2 6 1 0 4 8 5
6 3 8 5 9 1 2 0 3 8 6 1 6 9
4 5 2 9 4 0 2 0 6 8 9 4 1 3
5 7 6 2 8 9 4 3 1 8 4 0 6 1
1 3 0 6 7 2 9 4 6 0 3 6 5 2
6 8 2 0 5 6 2 7 4 1 9 4 8 3
2 6 0 9 4 8 2 1 3 4 5 6 2 9
```

Unless you are demonstrating how to analyze data, it is your job to make sense of the presented numbers for your learners. At the very least, make it easy for them to digest the information. Help learners see the pattern that aligns with what you are teaching. For example, if your goal is to help your audience identify how many times the number 7 appears, highlight it. Draw your learner's attention to the point you are making (Figure 5-24).

Figure 5-24. Highlighting What's Important

```
2 5 0 3 8 1 3 5 6 9 2 9 9 4
3 9 3 2 7 4 1 2 4 9 0 6 4 0
4 0 4 8 2 0 1 0 4 8 6 7 2 3
2 0 5 6 5 9 1 2 0 2 1 4 6 5
8 6 3 7 6 3 6 2 2 8 3 5 0 6
9 0 4 5 6 6 9 2 8 1 0 5 4 9
3 9 4 6 1 9 2 0 2 0 4 5 7 5
1 0 4 5 6 9 0 2 6 1 0 4 8 5
6 3 8 5 9 1 2 0 3 8 6 1 6 9
4 5 2 9 4 0 2 0 6 8 9 4 1 3
5 7 6 2 8 9 4 3 1 8 4 0 6 1
1 3 0 6 7 2 9 4 6 0 3 6 5 2
6 8 2 0 5 6 2 7 4 1 9 4 8 3
2 6 0 9 4 8 2 1 3 4 5 6 2 9
```

In most instances, you have already done the analysis, and your intent is to explain the presented data as they pertain to the subject matter and your audience. Almost all data visualization assumes some level of analysis has occurred, and the goal is to make informed decisions with the results. In these cases, you want to show the relevant data only, reduce clutter, and use verbal, textual, and visual cues to explain your content. Put data into a context that your audience cares about. Tell a story about it. For example, Figure 5-25 places the number 7 into context, and the supporting text tells a quick story about why it matters and how it came to be. Alternatively, the presenter could also show the number 7 only and say what is written in the text. By showing the number without immediate explanation, you will prompt your audience to look to you for the rest of the story.

Figure 5-25. Getting to the Point of the Data

Apply these principles to all quantitative charts to help your audience see your point. For example, if you want to focus on one data series, highlight it by reducing the relative contrast on other data, as shown in these before and after charts (Figure 5-26).

Even better, get to the point. Make it clear why are you showing the chart (Figure 5-27). Your audience expects you to have done the analysis and are looking to you—the expert—for answers.

[
"Easily format every element on a chart using [the] Chart Elements drop-down under the Format tab in the Current Selection area."

—Glenna Shaw, Microsoft PowerPoint MVP
]

Figure 5-26. Before and After

Before

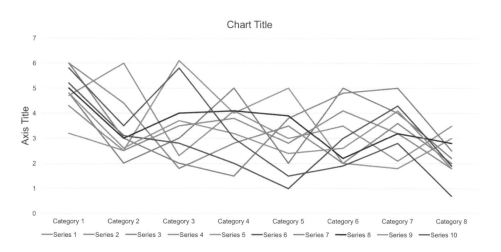

After

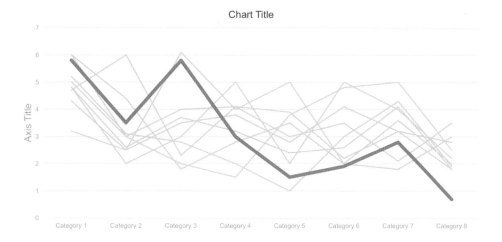

Figure 5-27. Getting to the Point With Backup Data

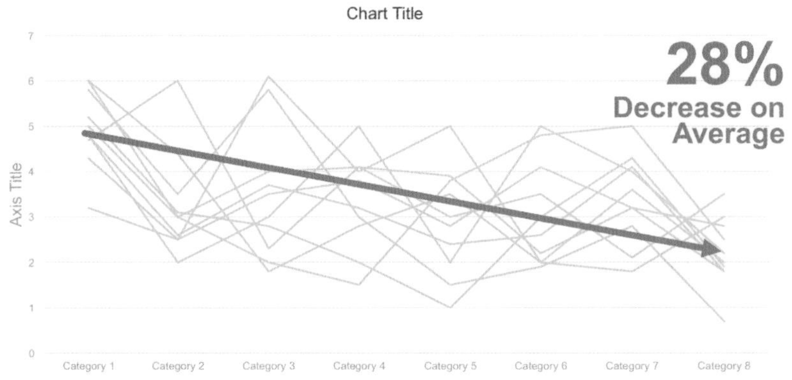

"When I see a presentation full of unreadable graphs and tables, I think, 'Wow, this person sure wants me to see how hard he worked to crunch all these numbers.' We're not in third grade, and I don't need you to show me your work . . . show me what's relevant and tell me what your point is. If you think I'll want detailed background info, then give me that in a leave-behind because I can read your 12-point type on a sheet of paper. But I can't on the screen."

—Echo Swinford, Microsoft PowerPoint MVP

Keep your quantitative charts simple. As visual communications expert Edward Tufte (1983) advises, remove any unnecessary "chartjunk" like effects, 3-D, axes, legends, markings, and titles. Succinct, clear communication in any format—visual, text, or auditory—is professional.

When picking a chart, know that most quantitative charts can share the same information. Pick the best one to tell your story. In Figure 5-28, both charts contain the same information, but they convey it differently. The pie chart quickly compares proportional values, whereas the bar (or column) chart emphasizes numeric analysis.

Figure 5-28. Pie Versus Bar: Two Different Chart Types

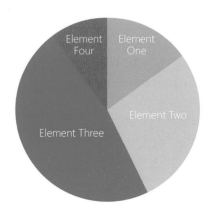
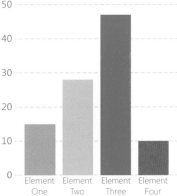

Photographs

Photographs elicit the strongest learner responses. Use photographs to support key messages, cement your content in reality, and engage your learners' memories and emotions. For example, if you are educating participants on a new potable water process, show before and after images to reinforce your goals. Share the results of bringing drinking water to people who desperately need it.

Tip: If you want to learn more (a lot more) about quantitative charts and diagrams, read Robert L. Harris's 1999 book, *Information Graphics: A Comprehensive Illustrated Reference*. It is an in-depth information graphic resource.

To add graphics and imagery to your slides, you have two choices: Build it or buy it. In chapter 4, you learned how to add your own photos. To buy stock visuals, video, and audio, check out the websites in Table 5-1.

Table 5-1. Websites for Stock Visuals, Video, and Audio

URL	Infographics	Quantitative Graphics	Symbols	Photographs	Video	Audio
GetMyGraphics.com	Yes*	Yes*	Yes*	Yes*	No	No
PresentationLoad.com	Yes*	Yes*	Yes*	Yes*	No	No
SlideShop.com	Yes*	Yes*	Yes*	Yes*	No	No

Table 5-1. Websites for Stock Visuals, Video, and Audio (cont.)

URL	Infographics	Quantitative Graphics	Symbols	Photographs	Video	Audio
TheNounProject.com	No	No	Yes*	No	No	No
iStockPhoto.com	Yes	Yes	Yes	Yes	Yes	No
DreamsTime.com	Yes	Yes	Yes	Yes	Yes	Yes
ShutterStock.com	Yes	Yes	Yes	Yes	Yes	Yes
Pexels.com	No	No	No	Yes	No	No
BigStockPhoto.com	Yes	Yes	Yes	Yes	Yes	No
ThinkStockPhotos.com	Yes	Yes	Yes	Yes	No	No
Stock.Adobe.com	Yes	Yes	Yes	Yes	Yes	No

*PowerPoint native files. TheNounProject.com includes .svg files that are editable in newer versions of PowerPoint.

In Figure 5-29, I used one photograph to explain three concepts. The objects in the room represented different aspects of our solution. To create this effect, I placed a full-screen rectangle over the photo. I then changed the opacity of the rectangle so that I could see my photograph. Next, I used the Freeform shape tool to outline the object I wanted to highlight. Using Merge (or Combine) Shapes, I subtracted the Freeform shape (outline) from the rectangle. Finally, I modified the color and added icons with text to support my message.

Figure 5-29. One Photograph, Three Messages

Summary

Follow as much of the process as you can for the Design phase. As with the Discover phase, focus and spend more time on the areas that benefit you most. If you only have time for one thing, the most important step in the process is having a motivational takeaway. Skipping this step ensures your presentation is destined to be ignored and forgotten.

Storyboarding saves time. I help large and small corporations develop four- to eight-hour presentations meant to demonstrate new products and upgrades to customers and prospects. When I'm first brought in on new projects, the team tells me about the project and wants to see results as quickly as possible. I explain the benefits of storyboarding and, to date, everyone agrees. I spend time storyboarding and then we meet again. I walk the team through the sketches to get feedback. If the feedback requires me to make extensive changes, I resketch and present it again. If the edits are light, I begin rendering using the storyboard and their input.

Choose your look and feel carefully. The learner's elephant—their emotional, unconscious mind—immediately reacts to aesthetic choices such as color, style, and imagery. Your participants will absolutely judge your content by its design. If you use quality design, they'll assume that you have quality content. Use aesthetics to influence, motivate, and guide their elephant to improve the likelihood of success.

Here's a checklist for PowerPoint design principles:

- ☐ **Learn and apply the design principles.**
- ☐ **Learn key PowerPoint features.**
- ☐ **Practice and give yourself projects.**
- ☐ **Buy or build what you need.**
- ☐ **Make an inspiration file.**

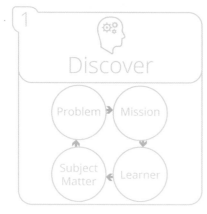

1

Discover

Problem → Mission

Subject Matter ← Learner

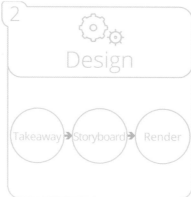

2

Design

Takeaway → Storyboard → Render

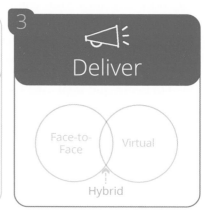

3

Deliver

Face-to-Face   Virtual

Hybrid

Phase 3
Deliver

No matter how your presentation is delivered, think of it as a conversation—not a monologue. For example, asking a rhetorical question during the presentation prompts your learners' brains to reply—an internal dialogue. Even in a lecture, their minds should be asking questions that your next sentence, slide, or section answers.

You want your audience interested and engaged. You want their minds active and eager. Learning how experienced presenters prepare and deliver presentations is the secret to their success.

There are many delivery best practices that apply to face-to-face, virtual, and hybrid presentations. And there are techniques that pertain specifically to one or the other. Knowing the best approaches to each technique is the purpose of phase 3: Deliver.

But this phase is for you even if you are not the presenter. Understanding the right way to present will help you make better PowerPoint content. Seeing your content from the perspective of a presenter will inform the choices you make in the Discovery and Design phases.

6

10 Best PowerPoint Delivery Practices

ach time I present, I learn something new. At this stage in my career, it's usually what *not* to do. Having watched hundreds of presentations at many conferences and learning events, I learn from others as well. When I see something fantastic, I weave what I learn into the best practices I test and share. The same is true when I participate in a presentation that misses the mark. For instance, during a keynote at a conference I attended, the presenter incorrectly used industry terms. Learners thought he wasn't sincere and didn't understand their world, and his message was partially lost as a result.

Another time, I watched a presenter cover the projector with a piece of paper to prevent the audience from seeing his slide. (He could have clicked the *B* key to make the screen turn black.) The bulb overheated and blew. We then spent 15 minutes waiting for a replacement bulb while the presenter grew more and more frustrated.

I want to ensure I do the best job possible, avoid flubs and gaffes, and know what to do when the unexpected happens. I suspect you do too. For this reason, I have assembled the most important best practices for delivering all types of PowerPoint presentations.

This chapter focuses on the 10 critical factors that the best-of-the-best PowerPoint training events share to ensure success.

Write Your Script (or Speaker Notes) Before Practicing

Use this as an opportunity to decide how to talk about your message. In your own voice, make it as perfect as you can. Writing your narrative helps hone your words and makes your presentation succinct, clear, and easy to follow.

Once you are happy with what you have written, read it out loud and edit as needed. Repeat this step until it sounds perfect to you and is comfortable for you to say.

At any point, you can add your script to the PowerPoint Notes pane. The Notes pane is a box that appears below each slide. To add your script, simply write or copy and paste your notes in this area. Your Notes pane is available in Presenter View. In this view, it is only seen by the presenter. To access Presenter View, choose Slide Show and then right-click on your screen and select Use Presenter View.

> "'Too many words' happens both on slides and in speech. Like designers applying white space in layouts, speakers can and should embrace silence—in the right length at the right places—to emphasize certain words and phrases."
>
> —Tony Ramos, The Presentationist

Next, try going through your slides without your notes. Don't worry about saying the words exactly as written. Use what you wrote as a guideline and practice your timing. Even if you forget the perfect way to say it, it doesn't matter. Your words should flow naturally and honestly, and the script should cover the most important points you wanted to make.

It's acceptable to use notes, especially for virtual events. However, skilled presenters speak from experience without notes. They may have cues or reminders placed on their podium or devices, but they will not read from note cards. The audience will more likely perceive you as an expert if you don't read from your notes.

Practice

To be specific, practice out loud. I may sound great in my head, but when I say it out loud, I often struggle. I trip over the words, mispronounce a term, or realize my message isn't clear. Every presentation book I have read encourages presenters to "practice, practice, practice."

I was a presentation coach on an important project for Xerox. As the team prepared their slides, individuals found quiet places to practice. I walked around and saw different approaches. Some worked through their slides in their minds, a few recited the text orally while sitting at their desks, and others stood and spoke to the room. When we reconvened as a group and presented in front of a live audience, the presenters who practiced out loud were comfortable and their delivery had improved. Those who practiced silently stumbled and often became frustrated.

Inevitably, the presentation will not go as planned. You may encounter technical issues or a learner who routinely interrupts the class with questions or comments. Being comfortable with your content makes it easy to solve a hiccup—you don't have to try to remember what you were supposed to say next after fixing the problem. It ensures you remain in control and the presentation flows smoothly despite disruptions.

Through practice, you will intuitively know where and when you can modify your presentation to accommodate the unexpected. For example, say you need to switch to a new projector, which eats away at your workshop schedule. What must you keep and what can you throw away? If you remember your presentation well, you know what can stay and what can go.

The best-case scenario is to practice in front of others. Re-enact the actual event to uncover any glitches, omissions, or hurdles before you present the final version. If you are using technology, test it. Know how it works and doesn't work. Try to break it. When you mess up (and you will), keep going. Everyone makes mistakes. Get comfortable with slips, blunders, and gaffes. If it is an obvious misstep, lightly acknowledge it and move forward. For example, in your personal life, you've likely made a mistake while chatting with a friend. What did you do? Did you get upset and leave or did you acknowledge it (maybe laughing) and move forward? A presentation is no different. Mistakes are OK; don't make a big deal about them and your audience won't either.

Be Passionate

This requires an emotional commitment. It creates contagious enthusiasm. Your level of interest transfers to your learners. Great trainers and facilitators have an intense, compelling conviction for sharing their topic. They believe it will help their participants achieve their goals.

My success rate is high and my reviews are among the best-of-the-best. I'm not sharing this to brag; there are many trainers and facilitators who are much (much, much, much) smarter and more skilled than I am. But my energy and excitement are applauded in reviews, and that energy is a result of my

"When your heart is racing, it feels as if you are in a runaway car with no control at all. But no matter how nervous you are, there is always one thing you *can* control: the pace at which you speak. This is not a skill . . . it is just a matter of conscious thought—speak more slowly! When you do that, you give yourself the chance of slowing everything down, and . . . you can regain control. Then you can breathe, pause, and gesture. And all of that contributes to the further slowing of your pace. This can all snowball for the good . . . and it can truly start with you reminding yourself to speak more slowly."

—Rick Altman,
Author, *Why Most PowerPoint Presentations Suck*,
Founder of the Presentation Summit

passion. It is evident in every slide, word, and gesture in my class. Being a great educator is not a job; it's a calling. Having a passion for your content coupled with a strong desire to support others will catapult your PowerPoint presentations to new heights.

Be Yourself

People trust people who seem genuine, so show that you care: Smile. Laugh. Get excited! Be animated when it makes sense and feels right. If you are nervous, be honest. I once spoke as part of an "Ignite" at a conference. An Ignite is a sequence of five-minute presentations, where each presenter must use 20 slides that auto-advance every 15 seconds. I was so nervous because the format was new to me, and I was not shy about sharing my anxiety. I embraced it and didn't panic. The presentation went well and no one seemed to mind how worried I was, maybe because they could relate to my anxiety.

You are not expected to be perfect. Mistakes happen to everyone. If you roll with the issue, so will your learners. For example, at times I lose my place because I'm excited about a topic. I laugh and ask someone, "Where was I?" They tell me and we are back on track. If I get upset, my audience feels it. If I'm genuinely excited and happy to be there, my learners feel that too.

Use a Delivery Pattern Interrupt

If you have a nervous habit, such as stammering, repeatedly saying certain words, or putting your hands in your pockets, use a pattern interrupt to stop bad behavior. Replace an unconscious impulse with a conscious thought, and over time, you will see your performance improve.

"Don't be afraid of a moment of silence while you gather your thoughts or check your notes. It may feel awkward to you, but it won't to the audience."

—Echo Swinford, Microsoft PowerPoint MVP

For example, anxiety often causes presenters to want to fill silence with words and sounds like *um*, *ah*, *y'know*, or *OK*. To avoid this, practice out loud and every time you start to utter one of those words, say "one." Do this until you are consistently saying "one" instead of the other filler words. Next, every time you would speak "one" aloud, say it in your mind. Now, you sound wise. To your audience, it sounds as if you are pausing to pick the right words to say.

Use a pattern interrupt to replace one behavior with another. It takes time, but eventually, the new desired action becomes habit and requires no effort at all. Stick with it and you will become a better presenter.

Use a Checklist

Make a list of everything you need for your presentation. Include items like files, learning materials, props, electronic equipment, giveaways, assessments, and tests.

Test Everything

Arrive early—the earlier the better—and test everything. Make sure your projector, slides, software, polls, audio, video, links, and so on are operating as expected. When I was teaching a class in Savannah, Georgia, I arrived 30 minutes early and realized I'd forgotten my adapter to plug my laptop into the projector. Because I didn't have a backup plan, I had to solve a big problem minutes before starting. Ultimately, I shared my blunder with the audience, transferred the slides to a friend's laptop, and started three minutes late. (I've learned to always keep a copy of my presentation on a universal hard drive.)

For face-to-face and hybrid presentations, make sure equipment is working the way you want it to. The number one thing I check is whether the laptop is showing my presentation as expected. For example, perhaps the projector is set to a 4:3 aspect ratio, and your slides are set to 16:9. I also often need to optimize the projector's brightness and contrast for the room's lighting.

For virtual presentations, test critical elements before starting, such as your audio and slides. If you are using video, polls, breakout rooms, whiteboards, or any other interactive features, make sure they work, too. I prefer to log in 30 minutes early to fix any technical hiccups.

Depending upon which software you choose, be aware that some PowerPoint effects, such as animation and transparency, do not function when presented online. Uncover what does and doesn't work in a virtual setting before making and presenting your slides. (See the virtual and hybrid delivery sections in chapter 7 for more information.)

Have a Backup Plan

Always have another option ready to go in the event the unexpected occurs. Sometimes a backup plan is as simple as postponing the event, or it could be as drastic as ditching your PowerPoint file altogether.

In my years as an educator, I've experienced technology and power failures, truncated or extended timelines, language barriers, attendee arguments, hecklers, and injuries. For instance, I was once teaching a class about government and commercial proposal development. Part of the class involved playing proposal Pictionary. The game requires a volunteer to pick a game card with a key term and then draw it on a flipchart while the audience tries to guess the word.

Unfortunately, I forgot to bring the cards. The backup plan I used was to whisper a word to a volunteer. The game then proceeded normally. Now, I carry a spare set of game cards in my travel bag with my computer.

Respect Your Audience

They're taking time from their busy schedules to attend your PowerPoint presentation, so don't waste it. Just like you, they are experts at what they do. Appreciate and welcome their expertise, treat them with kindness, and hold them in high regard. Your audience can sense your attitude. Respect goes both ways; a lack of respect for your audience will undermine your credibility and impede your success.

When appropriate, introduce yourself and learn your participants' names. Once you know their names, use them. Calling participants by name is professional, engages your audience, avoids confusion, and builds trust.

As shown in Figure 6-1, for face-to-face and hybrid classes, I create a seating chart and spell names phonetically.

Figure 6-1. Class Seating Chart

You are the host, so welcome your audience and make them feel comfortable. Set the pace and tone and manage expectations. Make the rules, but get approval from your learners. For example, before the class (or just as it begins), I set the tone by asking everyone what they hope to get out of the class. In front of the class, I write their answers on a flipchart. Their responses act as a checklist at the end of the presentation to ensure we covered the topics and issues that everyone requested. If we won't cover a learner's request, I manage expectations up front and offer to meet during breaks or at lunch to review their questions. I may even add that topic to my next presentation.

When the class officially starts, I share how the class works. I explain that this is not a formal class, but an interactive one. It's a dialogue between smart people, so if anyone has a question at any time, they should ask it. I encourage them to shout it out, raise their hand, or do whatever is comfortable for them.

Before our first break, I say, "Let's have a little fun. If you are late returning from break, you either sing one line from your favorite song or tell us a 30-second funny story about yourself. Give me a thumbs-up if you are OK with this. I kinda hope someone is late." (I say the last sentence in a lower volume.)

Demonstrate that you provide a safe place for your learners—a place where participation is rewarded. For example, do not ask, "Who doesn't know what a dashboard graphic is?" Attendees who do not know may feel demeaned and too awkward to admit their ignorance to an entire class. Instead, ask, "Who knows what a dashboard graphic is?" Now, you're protecting your learners. Thank them for contributing.

Engage

All expert trainers and facilitators engage learners. Interactive challenges are good strategies, but there are other techniques that can pull your audience into your presentation. Consider these surefire approaches:

Surprises

Do something unexpected. The human brain pays attention to things that are different; if attendees think they know what you will do before you do it, they tune out. It can be as simple as suddenly lowering or raising your voice or showing an unexpected image. The only rule is to make sure your surprise is germane to your point. Human brains like to be surprised—especially when we feel safe.

Stories

Tell a story. A good story engages your audience by activating various parts of their brains. I recommend personal stories because they are easy to remember and increase learner empathy. The story should enhance your message and not stray off topic. Again, practice delivering your story for maximum impact.

There are many storytelling techniques, but they all have one thing in common: a beginning, a middle, and an end. To learn more about storytelling, consider Robert McKee's 1997 book, *Story: Substance, Structure, Style, and the Principles of Screenwriting.*

Use one of these starting points when telling a story: Start your story with little to no introduction. Your audience is on a ride and unconsciously they will try to figure out where you are going. Or, state a fact to give your learners a reason to care about your story. For example, you might say, "I made $50,000 in one hour doing one thing differently." Alternatively, you might ask a question, "Have you ever forgotten why you walked into a room? Do you want to know why it happens and what you can do about it?"

Your story should have a logical flow, with one event leading to the next and a purpose behind every event and word. If you forget a portion of the story, weave it in. Avoid saying, "Oh yeah, I forgot something. . . ." For example, you could say, "Little did they know that one week ago I had [done what I forgot to share earlier in my story]."

Keep your ending simple and concise and tie it into one takeaway—a single takeaway is more likely to be remembered than several.

Questions

Try these prompts to solicit a spoken or unspoken answer to a question:

- Ask a volunteer to reply.
- Ask the class to discuss their answers to a question.
- Share a rhetorical question.
- Request a show of hands.
- Conduct a live or online poll.
- Ask for a volunteer to share their opinion or experience.

Games

Find or create a game to reinforce an important point, to teach a skill, or as a demonstration. For example, to help learners remember the relative value of sales activities, I made a variation of the card game War. I created multiple sets of 10 cards, each with a different sales activity and a unique number (Figure 6-2). Higher numbers equal higher-value sales activities and trump lower-level actions. Every attendee is given 10 cards and asked to play the game with the person to their left. Each player lays down a card, and the player with the higher-value card keeps both cards. Eventually, one player has all the cards. The game, through repetition and unconscious learning, helps the audience remember the sales activities with the greatest likelihood of success.

Figure 6-2. Card Game Examples

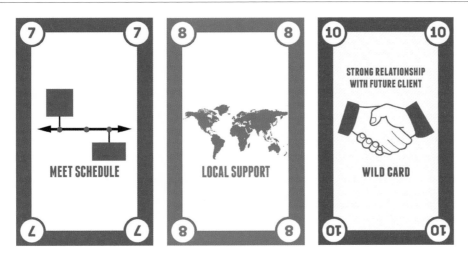

When creating games, I recommend keeping the exercise as simple as possible and leveraging an activity that is familiar to your audience. Complex exercises can be confusing and detract from the game's purpose. Complexity is relative; know your learners' proficiency before designing a game. For example, an activity based on mah-jongg may be too difficult for most to learn during the time allotted, but it could be appropriate for specific audiences.

Props

Physical objects involve more senses, and they activate different parts of your learners' minds. I use props in a number of ways. For some classes, I toss a beach ball to audience members to pick volunteers. In other learning events, I use an object to determine who has the right to talk, such as a "talking stick." Props can include models, toys, balloons, gadgets, animals, and anything that improves learning.

You can also ask attendees to bring an item to share with the class that is related to your presentation. In one of my classes, an attendee once brought examples of his marketing documents to show us.

Be creative. Any object can become a prop as long as it is relevant, engages your audience, and helps them learn. At a TED Talk, Bill Gates once released mosquitoes into the auditorium to reinforce the fact that poverty-stricken nations suffer from the highest counts of malaria. After the insects flew into the audience, he said, "There's no reason only poor people should have the experience." Attendees laughed, safe in the assumption that those mosquitoes were malaria-free (Gates 2009).

My dad is a magician. He sometimes says, "At the end of this trick, I will show you something that no one on the planet Earth has ever seen before. No kings, queens, or presidents in the history of the world. Neither the richest person nor the most powerful ruler has ever seen this. You will be the first person on the globe to see it." At the end of his routine, he reaches into his pocket and pulls out an unshelled peanut. He opens it and holds up the peanut inside, then announces, "No one has ever seen this exact peanut, and no one will ever see it again." He then eats it.

However, do not use props as entertainment only; they must bring value. Avoid using too many props, and test them before your presentation: Make sure the batteries are charged, the sound works, and they function as expected. Keep them hidden for an added element of surprise, and put them away when you're finished to prevent distraction.

Although not as effective, props also work virtually. For example, you could show a photograph or share a video of the object. You can toss an electronic ball, pass a digital talking stick, and play a video of a new peanut being opened. Sharing the props in an unexpected way will keep your audience engaged.

Solve a Problem

Challenges are deeply engaging, so give your learners tests, quizzes, puzzles, riddles, or scenarios to navigate. The activity should clearly support the learning objectives. In my presentation psychology classes, I ask attendees to create and present a two-slide PowerPoint presentation to convince every audience member to give them $1. (The problem: how to get $1 from each attendee.) The results are amazing; their presentation tactics and slides range from charitable donations to bribes. But the successful presentations offered something to the audience worth more than the dollar. For instance, one person said that if everyone gave him $1, he would purchase and deliver a bouquet of flowers to an attendee who recently lost their mother. Others made emotional appeals to inspire charitable donations.

Reward

Offer a reward for an accomplishment. The reward can be bragging rights, gift cards, money, trophies, and so on. Rewards activate the pleasure center in your learners' brains and release chemicals that make them feel good (that is, endorphins, dopamine, serotonin, and oxytocin).

An audience that feels good is more likely to learn. Depending upon the perceived value of the giveaway, it can also incentivize your audience to pay closer attention. During one of my classes, we watch PowerPoint videos. At the end of the video, I ask questions to see how closely everyone watched and listened. For each correct answer, they get a prize. Depending upon the nature of the class, questions can be about the topic or odd facts:

- What is the third step and how does it help you?
- How much time did Sarah say she saved using the new process?
- What color was the man's tie?
- What was first thing the narrator said?
- Who spoke first?

Additional Tips and Tools

When you develop your PowerPoint content, identify key success factors that you want your audience to remember. Use one of the seven engagement methods in this chapter to punctuate and highlight your message and improve retention.

Although it's rare, sometimes I have the luxury of having a producer—someone focused on the technical aspect of my presentation. The presentation team, be it multiple presenters or a presenter and a producer, are seen as one, meaning that as long as responsibilities are clear and the appropriate person knows and uses the best practices, you are safe. It is a collaborative process in these cases.

Humor is another tool you can use to engage your audience. I didn't include it in the list because it is a risky option; what you find funny may not be amusing to others. I often see cartoons inserted into PowerPoint presentations. Excluding copyright issues, the comics can be difficult to read and can be seen as a presentation trope or cliché.

Humor is subjective and can be off-putting. I was once working with a large company; during a stand-up meeting, the presenter shared a meme on his first slide that he had seen earlier that day. Some chuckled, but everyone agreed that it was "HR worthy"—funny to the presenter, but offensive to others. Levity can also be unsuitable for serious subjects and incongruous for certain audiences. Use comic relief carefully to avoid offense or making your learners uncomfortable. If you choose to use humor, be prepared to fail sometimes. You will make mistakes. Learn from your errors, and over time you will find the right balance.

> Tip: Keep your story active. When developing your slides, imagine the learner actively doing what you are teaching. Remove words like *will* and *shall* to bring the future into the present.

You can always improve. When your presentation is finished, ask for comments. Request honest attendee feedback and review it. Be specific; ask direct questions to uncover what elements were well received, and what discussions or exercises could improve. At the end of my PowerPoint sessions, I often distribute evaluation sheets, like those seen in Figure 6-3.

Figure 6-3. Evaluation Sheet Examples

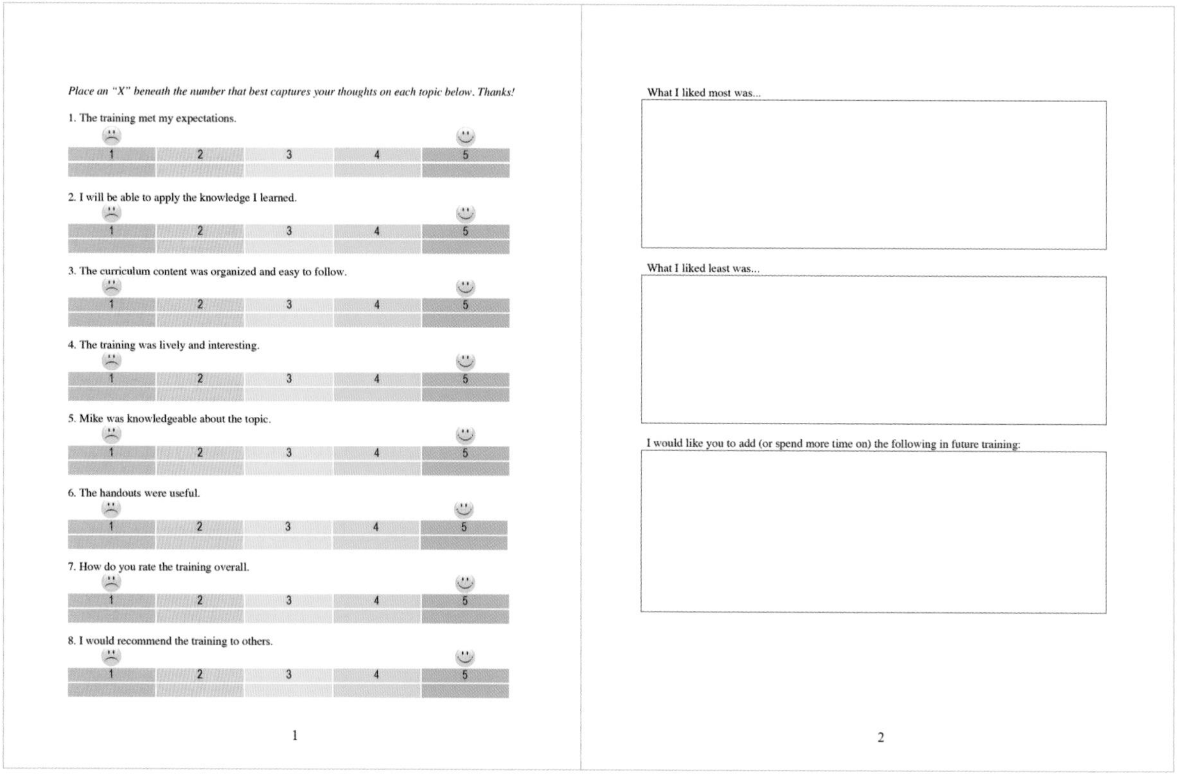

Place an "X" beneath the number that best captures your thoughts on each topic below. Thanks!

1. The training met my expectations.

| 1 | 2 | 3 | 4 | 5 |

2. I will be able to apply the knowledge I learned.

| 1 | 2 | 3 | 4 | 5 |

3. The curriculum content was organized and easy to follow.

| 1 | 2 | 3 | 4 | 5 |

4. The training was lively and interesting.

| 1 | 2 | 3 | 4 | 5 |

5. Mike was knowledgeable about the topic.

| 1 | 2 | 3 | 4 | 5 |

6. The handouts were useful.

| 1 | 2 | 3 | 4 | 5 |

7. How do you rate the training overall.

| 1 | 2 | 3 | 4 | 5 |

8. I would recommend the training to others.

| 1 | 2 | 3 | 4 | 5 |

1

What I liked most was...

What I liked least was...

I would like you to add (or spend more time on) the following in future training:

2

Summary

Learn from your and others' successes and failures, and apply these overarching delivery best practices for your PowerPoint presentations. There is always room for improvement. To this day, when I'm talking fast, I fall prey to an unconscious ah where I'd typically pause—especially on webinars. When I become aware of this action, I immediately incorporate one or more of the techniques I shared with you.

When developing your content and slides, think of ways to engage your audience based on what you have learned here. Find ways to weave in provocative questions, challenges, surprises, and games where it makes sense. Focus on the slides that need emphasis.

Here is a checklist of the 10 delivery best practices:

- ☐ **Write your script.**
- ☐ **Practice out loud.**
- ☐ **Be passionate.**
- ☐ **Be yourself.**
- ☐ **Use a pattern interrupt to correct your tics.**
- ☐ **Use a checklist to ensure you have everything you need.**
- ☐ **Test everything before using it.**
- ☐ **Have a backup plan.**
- ☐ **Respect your audience.**
- ☐ **Engage your audience.**

7

Delivering Your PowerPoint Presentation

ow, it's time to deliver your PowerPoint presentation. In this chapter, we look at delivering face-to-face, virtual, and hybrid presentations. Face-to-face presentations are live, where the learners and educator are physically sharing the same space. Virtual presentations are conducted online through web-sharing portals and videos. They can include recorded training modules, or be live or recorded. Hybrid presentations are a combination of the two:

- The instructor is face-to-face with part of the audience. Other learners are attending virtually.
- The instructor is virtual, and the entire class is in one central location.
- The instructor is virtual, and there are groups of participants in several locations.

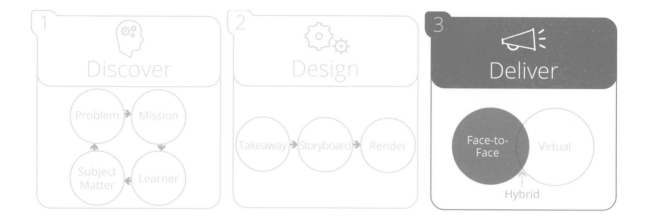

10 Strategies for Presenting Face-to-Face

For me, presenting live evokes the most anxiety. Fear itself can cause that which I dread the most: looking foolish, forgetting what I wanted to say, or a technical issue from which I cannot recover. I want to diminish my worries and be confident and comfortable. To do so, I practice and know my material. I have a backup plan and will walk the space before I present. I recommend you do the same.

For example, at the ATD 2017 International Conference & Exposition, I presented in an auditorium that seats almost 2,000 people. The layout and dynamics of a larger space is very different from those of a room designed for 300 or fewer. To be prepared, I asked for permission to enter the auditorium the day before. I walked the space by myself and checked my connections. I tested ways of moving through the space. I jumped on and off the stage to see how it felt. I presented out loud and imagined an audience. I made myself more comfortable with the space to eliminate as many new and unexpected variables as possible.

As suggested previously, practice out loud. Know your tics and fix them. Get comfortable with your material. Learn to present it nonlinearly should a problem arise. I have never had a class go as planned, but a backup strategy ensures you can manage the worst-case scenarios.

When possible, before the event begins, walk around the area. Practice your presentation in the environment or step through key moments in your mind while standing there. Become familiar with the space. Familiarity is comforting. Being prepared and comfortable with the space builds your confidence. It helps you navigate the inevitable eccentricities that arise.

In addition to the overall best practices, when it's time to give your live class, here are several in-person presentation rules to keep in mind:

Arrive Early

Give yourself time to set up, check the space, and modify, request, or acquire anything as needed. For example, the room may not be configured as you requested, or perhaps the projector hasn't been delivered yet. More time allows you to resolve issues with far less angst.

Know How to Adjust the Lighting and Sound

If your audience cannot clearly hear or see your content, your presentation will be less successful. When I arrive early, I test the audio and learn how to control the lights. (If AV professionals are present, work with them to set up the audio and visual equipment to your requirements.) No one enjoys constant buzzing, humming, or feedback, so make sure your audio is clear. Lighting helps control where your audience is looking. For example, during my presentation, lights are dimmed for maximum slide legibility, and during an exercise, they're brightened.

Know How to Resolve Technical Issues

What do you do in the event of a technological problem? Know whom to call for technical support. Keep the correct adapters for VGA or HDMI connections in case the facility does not supply them. Have extra batteries or know where to get them. Know how to contact technical support for a quick response. Be ready for anything—even if that means having a workaround in the event that technology fails. For instance, I once arrived early to set up for a workshop. I connected my computer to the projector and nothing happened; the projector did not sync with my computer. I tried every trick I knew, but nothing worked. Luckily, I had a copy of my PowerPoint presentation on an external drive. I copied the file to another computer, connected to the projector, and everything worked perfectly. Whew!

Move Around

Avoid being stationary, unless it is your preferred style or the situation requires it. Moving channels nervous energy. Walking through the space freely reminds your audience that you are comfortable being the host. If the event is being recorded, work with the videographer to know the safe zones so you do not leave the frame.

Do Not Read From Your Slides or Script

Attendees want you to be the expert. Reading from a script indicates that you aren't familiar with the material. Also, a lack of learner eye contact while scanning your pages stifles engagement. If you have text that is meant to be read, invite your audience to do so. When text appears on your slides and attendees read it to themselves, you are interrupting. If you want people to read the slide, ask them to take a moment to do so and then address the content.

Use Your Laptop or Monitor as a Prompter

In Slide Show, choose between standard view (Slide Show) or Presenter View. Standard view mirrors what is displayed on the projector, whereas Presenter View shows the current and upcoming slides, your speaker notes, presenter controls, and a timer. Alternatively, you can use cue cards or other notes, if needed. Choose what works best for you; it comes down to personal preference and the space. For example, if you don't have access to a teleprompter, then cue cards are best, if you need them.

You can further customize how your PowerPoint presentation is shown using the Slide Show tab. You can change monitors, present on two monitors, advance slides automatically, and much more under Slide Show. It is a simple interface and easy to learn.

Face Your Audience

Avoid turning your back to your learners. Walk backward, if you can. Would you turn your back to someone with whom you were speaking? I hope not. It's acceptable if it happens occasionally, but steer clear of frequently doing so out of respect for your learners. Watch their body language. If you see signs of disinterest, adjust your presentation as needed. For example, if I see that someone is distracted, I'll ask the audience a question and prompt that distracted learner to answer it.

Use Questions and Answers Effectively

They are important, and if you handle them well the class will get high marks. When you handle them poorly, it adversely affects your class. Manage your learners' expectations. In the beginning, tell them how and when to ask questions. When the learners ask questions, repeat or paraphrase them for the benefit of those who may have difficulty hearing. Respect the question no matter what it is about. The way you answer their question reminds everyone that this workshop is a safe place and all questions are welcome. If a question is asked that may derail the class, offer to discuss it during the next break.

Remember That Your Presentation Is a Conversation

The focus should be on you and not your slides. Slides support the presenter, not the other way around. If it is just a slide show, then why are you there?

Do Not Compete With Your Slides

When you want the focus to be anywhere else but your slides, click the *B* key, which will cause the screen to go black. Press the *B* key again to return to your normal screen.

Use this face-to-face checklist along with the other delivery checklists in this book:

- ☐ Arrive early.
- ☐ Know how to adjust the lighting and sound.
- ☐ Know how to resolve technical issues.
- ☐ Do not read from your slides or a script.
- ☐ Use notes for reference, if needed.
- ☐ Use Presenter View as a prompter, if needed.
- ☐ Move around.
- ☐ Face your audience.
- ☐ Repeat audience questions.

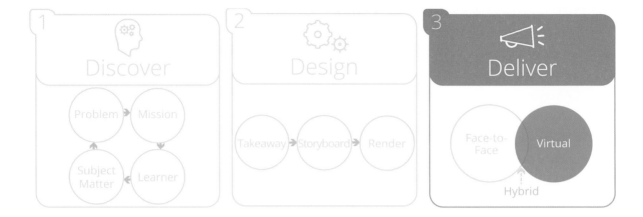

16 Strategies for Presenting Virtually

Make sure a virtual class is best for you and your topic. Presenting virtually has a lot in common with a face-to-face, live presentation, but there are fundamental differences. The number one benefit to an online class is that it is much easier for a geographically dispersed audience to attend. However, virtual presentations offer less learner feedback and engagement. During most virtual presentations, you can't see your audience, so interactivity requires technical proficiency. Plan ahead. Successful webinars take advantage of the technology.

In addition to the overall best practices, when it's time to give a virtual presentation, I keep in mind the following presentation rules.

Learn the Tool

Each webinar tool is unique, so get to know your tool before conducting a class. If it's the first time you or another presenter is using the tool, set up a practice presentation to work out the kinks before going live. Test the audio, video, image quality, animations, polls, and other interactive functionality. When selecting your tool, go to the company's website for a list of features. Some tools have built-in e-commerce and mailing list functions. Here's a list of popular webinar products:

- Adobe Connect (www.adobe.com/products/adobeconnect.html)
- AnyMeeting (www.anymeeting.com)
- Blackboard Collaborate (www.blackboard.com/online-collaborative-learning /blackboard-collaborate.aspx)
- Brainshark (www.brainshark.com)
- Cisco WebEx (www.webex.com)

- ClickMeeting (http://clickmeeting.com)
- EasyWebinars (http://easywebinar.com)
- Fuze (www.fuze.com)
- GoToTraining (www.gotomeeting.com/training)
- GoToWebinar (www.gotomeeting.com/webinar)
- iLinc (www.ilinc.com)
- Join.me (www.join.me)
- MeetingBurner (www.meetingburner.com)
- MegaMeeting (http://megameeting.com)
- Onstream (http://onstreammedia.com)
- ReadyTalk (www.readytalk.com)
- Skype (www.skype.com)
- WebinarIgnition (http://webinarignition.com)
- Webinars OnAir (www.webinarsonair.com)
- Zoom (http://zoom.us).

Have Your Login Credentials Handy

Have your access information available in case you lose your connection. The faster you log or call back in, the better.

Know How to Resolve Issues With the Tool

It could be as simple as having the technical support number. Be ready for things you know can go wrong. In one class I conducted, my animations didn't work, so I relaunched my presentation and the issue resolved itself. Your attitude sets the mood for your class. If you are frustrated, your participants may become anxious. For example, if an attendee has an issue, remain calm and ask them to log out and log back in, or follow any other procedures you use to resolve technical issues. The last resort is to share your webinar program's support number.

Share Protocols

Explain your agenda and other facts or events that will make audience involvement easier. Introduce and explain the features of the webinar tool to attendees. Share how to ask a question and use the whiteboard, and what to do if you or they are logged off or have technical issues. Ask attendees to demonstrate their understanding by having them test the chat function and other software features they are expected to use. When audio is involved, ask everyone to do a sound check. Ask attendees to indicate if they can hear you and confirm that you can hear them. Request that they mute themselves when they are not talking. List a series of requests at the beginning of the presentation to uncover questions and avoid disruptions later.

Use Quality Audio

Do not use your computer's built-in audio unless you have high bandwidth. I use either a landline or my cell phone with a headset. A headset keeps my hands free and delivers much better sound quality. Avoid voice over IP (VoIP) because it can degrade the quality of your sound and images by eating away at signal capacity. Mute attendees prior to starting to avoid background noise.

Use a Reliable, Fast Network

If you know that your connection is not dependable, find a quiet place with fast, predictable Internet access. When I'm at a hotel and need to give a webinar, I always pay for higher-speed access to avoid the challenges that arise from slow connection speeds. If you have limited bandwidth, avoid prolonged use of webcams. Use video as needed, but do not keep it on.

Present in a Safe, Quiet Place

Barking dogs, loud neighbors, sirens, doorbells, leaf blowers, lawn mowers, and other disruptions negatively affect the quality of your presentation. Think ahead and set up in a quiet location that is safe from interruptions. Deactivate any technology that may interfere with your session. For example, I turn off email and social media prompts and mute any nearby external devices that may ring, chirp, beep, or ding.

Start and End on Time

Begin and end your session at the times posted. Your learners are busy, so respect their time. If you start late or end before or after the posted time, manage expectations. Let everyone know the new timeframe and adhere to it. For example, if you are starting late, you can say, "For those who have already joined, we will start in two minutes to give our last few attendees an opportunity to log in." After a minute, announce, "We will begin in one minute so the last few attendees can log in." After the two minutes, start the presentation.

Have a Backup Computer, if Possible

Should your primary machine fail, be prepared. This is a costly option, but it is a lifesaver in those rare instances when technology fails.

Welcome Participants

Engaging your learners starts by welcoming them. I enter the webcast 30 minutes early to ensure an introductory slide appears on the screen when attendees log in. Verbally or textually welcome people either as they arrive or at predefined intervals, such as five minutes before class and as the session begins. Consider using an interactive activity such as an icebreaker. For example, during ATD Essentials Series classes, we ask attendees to point to their location on a map.

Build Seamless Interactivity Into Your Class

Interactivity during a virtual presentation, when done correctly, can be as effective as it is during a live event. The rule of thumb is to have some form of interactivity every third slide. Don't force it. It can be as simple as a hypothetical question and as involved as a breakout session, or when attendees are divided into self-contained working groups and given an assignment to complete. You can also provide keyboard or mouse controls to a learner.

Prompt Learners

Tell them what to do. I use a combination of verbal, graphic, and textual cues. For example, if I want my audience to select an object using their "pointer tool," I verbally ask them to do so, and in the upper left corner of my slide, a graphic and textual prompt appears (see the red corner in Figure 7-1).

Figure 7-1. Using a Slide With a Textual Cue

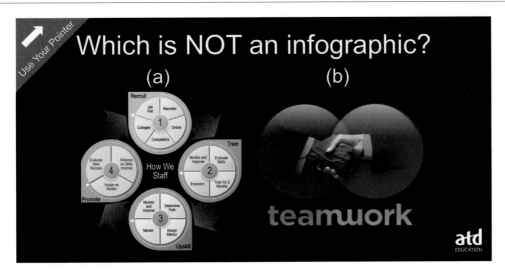

Recommend Using Individual Computers

To maximize engagement, you want everyone using their own computer. Sharing computers means each person takes turns interacting or one person acts for the group. As with a live class, the optimal solution is that everyone believes their voice can be or is heard.

Speak from your heart with the knowledge you have gained. Use your notes as prompts at first; as you become more comfortable, you won't need them. Practice and know your material. Unlike a face-to-face PowerPoint class, it is possible to read from a script without being seen; however, I do not recommend it. Reading text is different from speaking from your experience and understanding. It is difficult to hear and feel your passion when you are reading (or acting out) prewritten content.

Distribute Class Materials Ahead of Time

Most webinar tools offer the ability to share supplemental documents during the class. If you choose to distribute content during your event, build in time for download, technical hiccups, and review to prevent awkward pauses and interferences that affect engagement.

Print Your Slides and Use Them as a Guide

Print multiple slides on a page using the Handouts view. (In your print dialog box, under Layouts, select one of the Handouts options.)

Don't Use Your Webinar Tool for Quality Virtual Recordings

The recorded version can be less than ideal and unusable. If quality isn't critical, test your software before relying on this function. More learners are requesting training on demand—a prerecorded presentation that they can watch on their schedule. For on-demand training requests, review the Recording tool in chapter 4. Strive for good sound quality and clear messages and imagery, and include activities when possible. Provide supplemental downloads that support your learning objectives. When I'm nervous, it's easier for me to forget my initial steps, so I have set a reminder to click record before starting. For prerecorded presentations with activities, ask the viewer to pause the video and then return after the task is complete.

Use this virtual checklist along with the other delivery checklists in this book:
- ☐ Arrive early.
- ☐ Welcome attendees.
- ☐ Have your login credentials.
- ☐ Know how to resolve issues with the tool.
- ☐ Use notes for reference, if needed.

☐ Share protocols.

☐ Use quality audio.

☐ Use a reliable, fast network.

☐ Present in a safe, quiet place.

☐ Mute attendees prior to starting.

☐ If recording, select Record before beginning.

☐ Start and end on time or manage expectations.

☐ Use attendees' names.

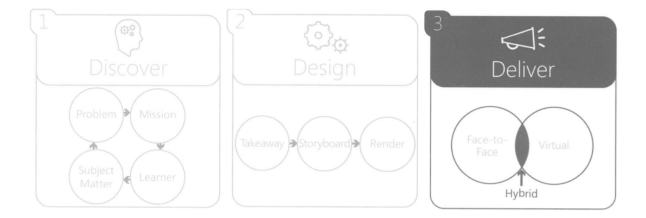

7 Strategies for a Hybrid Presentation

A hybrid presentation requires the best practices from both face-to-face and virtual presentations, with special considerations for remote participants. For mixed audiences, I design my PowerPoint for virtual attendees. For example, instead of a flipchart, I use an online whiteboard and recount things that occur locally for the benefit of remote participants. If only a physical flipchart is available, explain what learners are drawing or what you're writing down as it takes place.

When presenting hybrid PowerPoint presentations, it is easy to forget about remote learners. These attendees can feel left out and disengage without repeated "touches." It is your job to keep everyone on the same page and involved. Instant collocated interactions help us remain engaged. You want to find other ways to frequently engage everyone—especially remote attendees. Here are seven strategies for including all learners:

Create All-Inclusive Collaborative Exercises

For breakout groups, I ensure virtual learners work together through the webinar tool by pairing local with local and virtual with virtual.

Use Electronic Polls Instead of Written Ones

Alternatively, ask people to raise their hands—locally and electronically. Most online tools have a way for attendees to "raise their hand" or "flag a response." For hand raising with more than two options, I say, "Raise your hand if you choose A. Now, raise your hand if you choose B. And finally, raise your hand if you think C is the best option."

Share Graphics Onscreen

If a slide, graphic, or other project is being created in the physical environment, use your cell phone to share it onscreen. Before my class, I connect my cell phone to my laptop. During the event, I either take and display a picture with my phone or share my live camera feed. You can mirror your cell phone's screen with the right software. For Mac with an iPhone, I use QuickTime and select New Movie Recording. Then I choose my cell phone as the video input. For Windows, go to your favorite search engine and type "mirroring my cell phone in Windows." There are tips and tools that walk you through the process for your operating system and phone.

During exercises, if remote attendees cannot easily share a project they created by hand, I ask them to take a picture with their cell phone and text it to me. Once I have it, I share my screen with the class, because it is connected to my laptop.

Repeat or Paraphrase Questions

If remote attendees are confused, their attention wanes.

Use Webcams

Consider using a web camera so all participants can see you. Some webinar software gives you the option of splitting the screen between slides and video. However, be aware that video can degrade image and sound quality. Only choose this option if you have sufficient bandwidth.

Include Everyone

When asking for volunteers, include those not in the room—especially for answers to questions.

Do Not Mute the Audio

Let virtual participants speak when they want and solicit questions and input from them. For example, I'll ask the learners, "Do you have any questions?" and wait for those attending virtually. Sometimes, I specifically address those learners not in the room: "Dan, Aanya, Sarah, Antonio, do you have any questions?" Wait. Give them time to respond. Remote attendees tend to not speak for fear of talking over others or not being heard.

The secret is to involve everyone equally. Not being in the same room affects the connection those face-to-face immediately feel. Give particular attention to your remote learners. Accommodate them by frequently involving them throughout your PowerPoint presentation.

Use this hybrid checklist along with the other delivery checklists in this book:

☐ **Use all-inclusive exercises.**
☐ **Use interactive polls.**

☐ Share what is created in the class with everyone.

☐ Use a web camera, as needed.

☐ Involve remote attendees—a lot.

☐ Keep audio open for remote attendees.

Summary

Whether you are presenting face-to-face, virtually, or both, use these best practices to deliver an amazing PowerPoint presentation. The approaches I shared work, and I regularly use all the techniques. As a result, I'm less nervous because I feel prepared and ready for anything the presentation gremlins throw at me.

Afterword

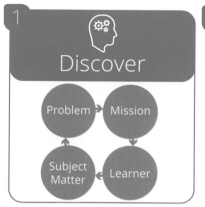
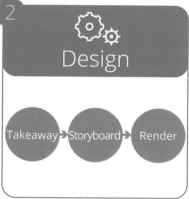
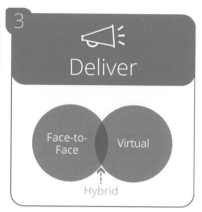

You are not done yet. Your journey is far from complete. You have one last hurdle to jump, one last enemy to slay—and that is you.

After I read a book or attend a class, I have learned a helpful new way of approaching my work. I think, "Wow! This is great. Where has this been all my life?" Then, when I return to my desk, I inevitably get swamped with work, and I go back to my old ways of doing things.

Fight the urge to do what is comfortable. Create new habits. Be willing to spend extra time up front applying what you have learned. It will save you money and time, and improve your success rate exponentially. Be willing to fail forward. Make mistakes and learn from them to improve. It's not only OK to mess up, but required. I learn more from failure than success.

You have the power to change the paradigm. You can end "death by PowerPoint," boring presentations and selfish seminars that alienate participants. The secret is to follow this (or a tailored version of this) process.

If you apply what you learned in this book, I promise that your PowerPoint presentations will be more effective, and as a result, you will expedite your personal success. Have the discipline to practice what you learned, and you will become a better PowerPoint presenter and achieve your professional goals faster.

In time, you will become a PowerPoint guru. Share what you've learned. Help others. Give back, and together we can change the world one presentation at a time.

Keep me posted. I want to know when you rock and when you don't. (If you don't fail, you aren't trying hard enough.) Email your stories and questions to Mike@BillionDollarGraphics.com.

Appendix A

Graphics help you explain complicated concepts and allow the audience to follow at their own speed. Use the following cheat sheets to pick the best graphic type. At its core, your graphic's message is communicating one of these 13 key concepts. Pick the concept that matches your message and then choose a graphic type under that concept.

Amount or Value

Simple
The information to be communicated is easy to understand and not involved.

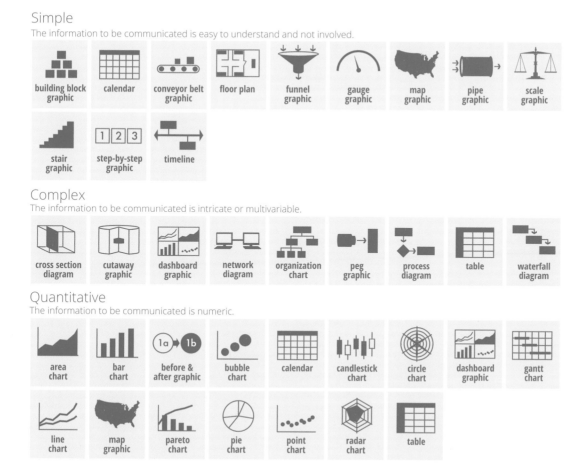

building block graphic · calendar · conveyor belt graphic · floor plan · funnel graphic · gauge graphic · map graphic · pipe graphic · scale graphic

stair graphic · step-by-step graphic · timeline

Complex
The information to be communicated is intricate or multivariable.

cross section diagram · cutaway graphic · dashboard graphic · network diagram · organization chart · peg graphic · process diagram · table · waterfall diagram

Quantitative
The information to be communicated is numeric.

area chart · bar chart · before & after graphic · bubble chart · calendar · candlestick chart · circle chart · dashboard graphic · gantt chart

line chart · map graphic · pareto chart · pie chart · point chart · radar chart · table

Architecture or Structure

Simple
The information to be communicated is easy to understand and not involved.

Complex
The information to be communicated is intricate or multivariable.

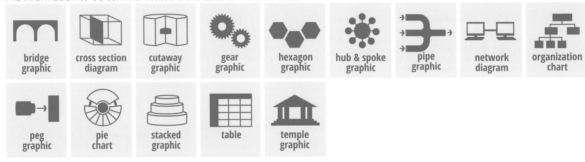

Quantitative
The information to be communicated is numeric.

Cause and Effect

Simple
The information to be communicated is easy to understand and not involved.

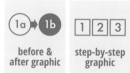

before & after graphic **step-by-step graphic**

Complex
The information to be communicated is intricate or multivariable.

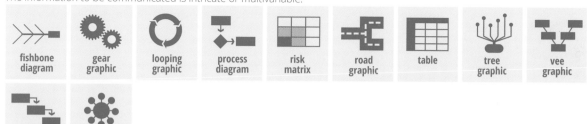

fishbone diagram **gear graphic** **looping graphic** **process diagram** **risk matrix** **road graphic** **table** **tree graphic** **vee graphic**

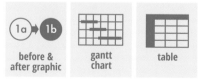

waterfall diagram **hub & spoke graphic**

Quantitative
The information to be communicated is numeric.

before & after graphic **gantt chart** **table**

Comparison

Simple
The information to be communicated is easy to understand and not involved.

| before & after graphic | gauge graphic | puzzle graphic | scale graphic | timeline |

Complex
The information to be communicated is intricate or multivariable.

| bridge graphic | dashboard graphic | table |

Quantitative
The information to be communicated is numeric.

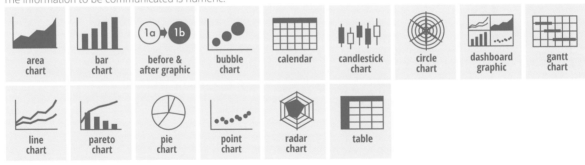

| area chart | bar chart | before & after graphic | bubble chart | calendar | candlestick chart | circle chart | dashboard graphic | gantt chart |

| line chart | pareto chart | pie chart | point chart | radar chart | table |

Hierarchy

Simple
The information to be communicated is easy to understand and not involved.

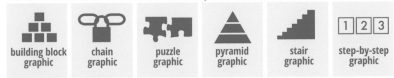

building block graphic   chain graphic   puzzle graphic   pyramid graphic   stair graphic   step-by-step graphic

Complex
The information to be communicated is intricate or multivariable.

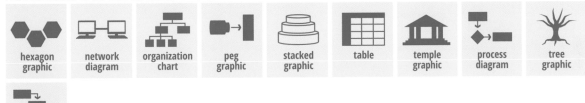

hexagon graphic   network diagram   organization chart   peg graphic   stacked graphic   table   temple graphic   process diagram   tree graphic

waterfall diagram

Quantitative
The information to be communicated is numeric.

table

Location or Distance

Simple
The information to be communicated is easy to understand and not involved.

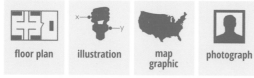

floor plan   illustration   map graphic   photograph

Complex
The information to be communicated is intricate or multivariable.

collage   road graphic   table

Quantitative
The information to be communicated is numeric.

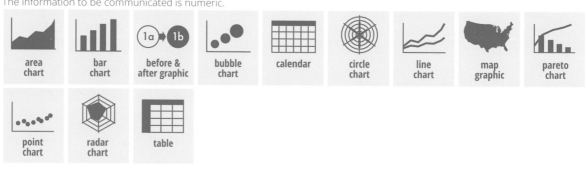

area chart   bar chart   before & after graphic   bubble chart   calendar   circle chart   line chart   map graphic   pareto chart

point chart   radar chart   table

Physical Description

Simple
The information to be communicated is easy to understand and not involved.

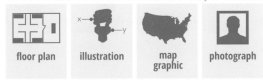

Complex
The information to be communicated is intricate or multivariable.

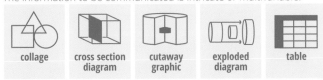

Quantative
The information to be communicated is numeric.

Process or Flow

Simple
The information to be communicated is easy to understand and not involved.

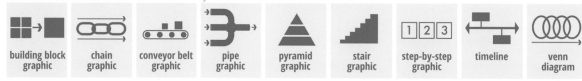

| building block graphic | chain graphic | conveyor belt graphic | pipe graphic | pyramid graphic | stair graphic | step-by-step graphic | timeline | venn diagram |

Complex
The information to be communicated is intricate or multivariable.

| bridge graphic | funnel graphic | gear graphic | looping graphic | spiral graphic | network diagram | pie chart | pipe graphic | process diagram |

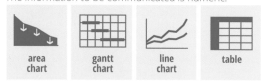

| road graphic | stacked graphic | vee graphic |

Quantitative
The information to be communicated is numeric.

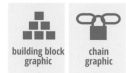

| area chart | gantt chart | line chart | table |

Protection or Isolation

Simple
The information to be communicated is easy to understand and not involved.

| building block graphic | chain graphic |

Complex
The information to be communicated is intricate or multivariable.

| cross section diagram | cutaway graphic | dome graphic | pipe graphic | stacked graphic |

Relationship

Simple
The information to be communicated is easy to understand and not involved.

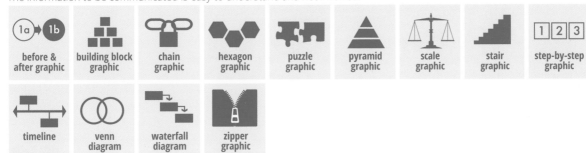

| before & after graphic | building block graphic | chain graphic | hexagon graphic | puzzle graphic | pyramid graphic | scale graphic | stair graphic | step-by-step graphic |

| timeline | venn diagram | waterfall diagram | zipper graphic |

Complex
The information to be communicated is intricate or multivariable.

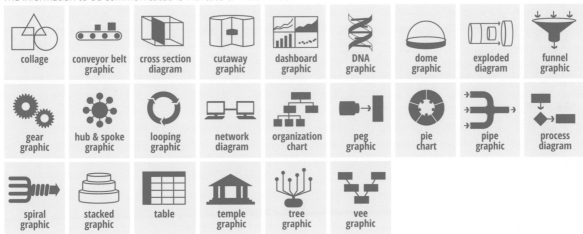

| collage | conveyor belt graphic | cross section diagram | cutaway graphic | dashboard graphic | DNA graphic | dome graphic | exploded diagram | funnel graphic |

| gear graphic | hub & spoke graphic | looping graphic | network diagram | organization chart | peg graphic | pie chart | pipe graphic | process diagram |

| spiral graphic | stacked graphic | table | temple graphic | tree graphic | vee graphic |

Quantitative
The information to be communicated is numeric.

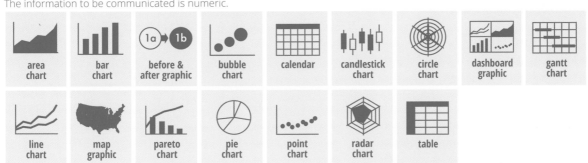

| area chart | bar chart | before & after graphic | bubble chart | calendar | candlestick chart | circle chart | dashboard graphic | gantt chart |

| line chart | map graphic | pareto chart | pie chart | point chart | radar chart | table |

Synergy

Simple
The information to be communicated is easy to understand and not involved.

building block graphic

chain graphic

puzzle graphic

pyramid graphic

venn diagram

zipper graphic

Complex
The information to be communicated is intricate or multivariable.

collage

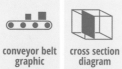
conveyor belt graphic

cross section diagram

cutaway graphic

dashboard graphic

DNA graphic

funnel graphic

gear graphic

hexagon graphic

looping graphic

organization chart

peg graphic

pie chart

pipe graphic

road graphic

spiral graphic

stacked graphic

temple graphic

vee graphic

Quantitative
The information to be communicated is numeric.

dashboard graphic

pie chart

Time

Simple
The information to be communicated is easy to understand and not involved.

before & after graphic

building block graphic

calendar

chain graphic

conveyor belt graphic

gauge graphic

pipe graphic

pyramid graphic

(stair graphic)
stair graphic

step-by-step graphic

timeline

Complex
The information to be communicated is intricate or multivariable.

bridge graphic

collage

dashboard graphic

process diagram

road graphic

spiral graphic

stacked graphic

table

tree graphic

waterfall diagram

Quantitative
The information to be communicated is numeric.

area chart

bar chart

before & after graphic

bubble chart

calendar

candlestick chart

circle chart

dashboard graphic

gantt chart

line chart

pareto chart

pie chart

point chart

radar chart

table

Transition

Simple

The information to be communicated is easy to understand and not involved.

before & after graphic · building block graphic · conveyor belt graphic · looping graphic · puzzle graphic · stair graphic · step-by-step graphic · timeline

Complex

The information to be communicated is intricate or multivariable.

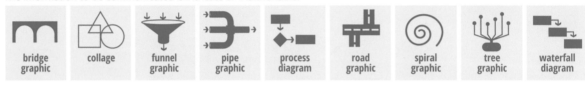

bridge graphic · collage · funnel graphic · pipe graphic · process diagram · road graphic · spiral graphic · tree graphic · waterfall diagram

Quantitative

The information to be communicated is numeric.

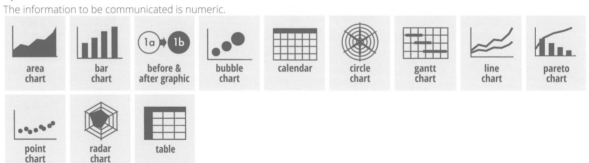

area chart · bar chart · before & after graphic · bubble chart · calendar · circle chart · gantt chart · line chart · pareto chart · point chart · radar chart · table

Appendix B

Use these step-by-step instructions to make commonly needed PowerPoint graphics. Using these techniques, you can make almost any visual element you can imagine. It also ensures that your content is 100 percent editable and has a low file size.

How to Make Gears in PowerPoint

1. Make a circle.

2. Make a 24-point star (or another star).

3. Increase the length of the star's points by selecting and moving the associated mode.

4. Select and center the circle and the star.

5. Select Merge Shape (or Combine Shape) and choose Intersect.

6. Draw a smaller circle. This will be the body of your gear.

7. Select and center the circle and the star.

8. Select Merge Shape (or Combine Shape) and choose Union.

9. Draw a smaller circle. This will be the center of your gear.

10. Select and center the central circle and the gear. Deselect all.

11. Select the gear shape first and then the center circle. Select Merge Shape and choose Subtract. The order of selection changes the outcome of the Merge effect.

12. If desired, choose Shape Fill/Picture or Texture Fill and select a metal texture. (Augment with a Gradient Outline.)

How to Make a Funnel in PowerPoint

1. Make an isosceles triangle.

2. Rotate 180 degrees.

3. Funnel Top: Draw an oval and duplicate it twice, for a total of three ovals. Draw a rectangle. Arrange as shown. If needed, choose Align Center for all objects.

4. Funnel Top: Select rectangle first and then oval 2. Select Merge Shape and choose Subtract. The order of selection changes the outcome of the Merge effect.

5. Funnel Top: Select the new shape and oval 3. Select Merge Shape and choose Union.

6. Funnel Top: Bring oval 1 down to rest on top of the new shape.

7. Funnel Bottom: Repeat steps 3-5, but with a taller rectangle and only two ovals.

8. Funnel Bottom: Select rectangle first and then oval 2. Select Merge Shape and choose Subtract.

9. Funnel Bottom: Select the new shape and oval 3. Select Merge Shape and choose Union.

10. Combine all elements as shown.

11. Draw a slightly smaller oval and place it at the top. This is the funnel opening.

12. Add color and gradient as desired.

How to Make a Gauge Graphic in PowerPoint

1. Draw a pie shape from Shapes/pie, and rotate the pie 90° clockwise. Use the Shift key when drawing a shape to ensure equal height and width.

2. Use the Reshape Tool to create a half-circle shape.

3. Draw an oval from Shapes/oval and position it as shown. If needed, align using Arrange/Align/Align Center.

4. Select both shapes. Use Merge Shapes, and then Union, to combine them all.

5. Make a pie chart with 20 equal segments, or however many segments you need for your gauge.

6. Align the pie chart with the gauge body.

7. Select individual segments and color as needed by using Shape Fill and Shape Outline. Use No Fill and No Outline for segments outside the gauge body.

8. Draw a triangle (for a gauge needle) and an oval. Scale and position as shown.

9. Duplicate the triangle, flip it 180° (or Arrange/Rotate/Flip Vertical), and align as shown.

10. Apply No Fill and No Outline to the bottom triangle, and group both triangles. This allows the gauge needle to rotate around the correct axis.

11. Bring the oval (the needle axis) to the front.

12. Add text, if desired. To rotate the needle, select it and use Arrange/Rotate/More Rotate Options and change Rotation.

How to Make a 3-D Conveyor Belt Graphic in PowerPoint

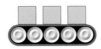

1. Conveyor Belt: Draw a rounded rectangle.

2. Conveyor Belt: Using the Reshape Tool, curve the edges as shown.

3. Conveyor Belt: Shape Fill black and apply a gray outline. Change the weight of the line as needed. The line weight is the thickness of your belt.

4. Wheels: Draw three circles of different sizes. Hold the Shift key to ensure circles are equal height and width. Choose Arrange/Align/Align Center/Align Middle.

5. Wheels: Apply a gradient fill: circle 1 = dark to light; circle 2 = light to dark; circle 3 = dark to light. Group all circles to make a wheel.

6. Wheels: Duplicate and select all wheels, with one wheel at either end of the conveyor belt. With all wheels selected, align as needed. Next, select Arrange/Align/Distribute Horizontally. Group all elements.

7. Boxes: Draw a rectangle and duplicate it. Position as shown.

8. Boxes: Color as desired, but remove the rectangle outlines. Group all elements.

9. With your conveyor belt graphic selected, choose Shape Format/Format Pane/3-D Rotation, and choose Off Axis 1 Right from the preset rotation options.

10. Choose Shape Format/3-D Format and enter the appropriate number for depth. The number is relative to the size of your conveyor belt. Modify as needed.

11. Select just the boxes and reduce the depth.

12. Reposition the boxes on the conveyor belt as shown. Add text as desired.

Glossary

A

Aesthetics: A set of principles regarding the nature and appreciation of beauty. The study of aesthetics increased the validity of many critical judgments concerning art. The established aesthetic principles create a shared vocabulary and understanding for the objective evaluation of beauty.

Analogy (visual): A depiction or explanation of an action, concept, or entity that augments (having a logical relevance to that which is augmented) another action, concept, or entity, making a comparison to improve communication. A visual analogy compares a variety of attributes. It is often used to form logical arguments: If two different things are similar in one way, they might be similar in other ways as well.

Animation: A set of effects that make objects appear, disappear, or move in Slide Show mode.

Area Chart: A graphic that depicts continuous quantitative data, usually over time, and uses filled areas to communicate amounts, timeframes, or values.

Author: The PowerPoint content creator.

B

Balance (visual): Balance is achieved when the visual "weight" of both halves of a slide or graphic is similar, giving a sense of equilibrium.

Bar Chart: A graphic that depicts the changes in quantitative data using "bars," where the size of each bar represents the proportional value of the quantitative data.

Before-and-After Graphic: A graphic that compares the "as is" or "before" state to the "to be" or "after" state.

Bridge Graphic: A graphic metaphor depicting the connection or transition between two actions, concepts, or entities.

Bubble Chart: A graphic that uses circles or spheres to show ranges of quantitative data. It can also illustrate the uncertainty of predicted value.

Building Blocks: A graphic that interconnects data to illustrate how elements work together to create a larger unit.

Bullet: A symbol that appears before a line of type, usually in a list, for emphasis.

C

Calendar: A table showing years (or a year), months, weeks, and days.

Candlestick Chart: A chart traditionally used to analyze values and sales of stocks, bonds, commodities, and so forth. The price is shown in the vertical axis, and time is shown in the horizontal axis.

Chunking: Breaking content into bite-sized pieces that can then be reassembled to show an overview of the content presented.

Circle Charts: A family of graphics that display quantitative data using a circular format and includes radar graphs, sector graphs, circle column graphs, and many similarly shaped graphics.

Cognitive Curiosity: Evoking the underlying motivation in learners to seek more information through investigation.

Cognitive Dissonance: Having inconsistent thoughts, beliefs, or attitudes. For presentations, doing or showing the unexpected.

Collage: A graphic that is composed of juxtaposed images.

Color: The hue, value, and saturation we see when we look at something.

Conceptualization: The process of creating a design or design plan. It often involves visualizing and graphically representing your content.

Conscious Communication: Intellectual comprehension of the information presented.

Conveyor Belt Graphic: A graphic metaphor that depicts a repeatable linear process.

Cross Section Diagram: A graphic where an entity or depiction of a concept is cut in half so the different layers that make up the whole can be viewed and individually defined.

Cutaway Diagram: This graphic is similar to a cross section diagram, where you can see the inner workings or mechanics of an entity or depiction of a concept viewed through a missing or transparent portion of the outermost layer.

D

Dancing Bologna: Gratuitous and distracting PowerPoint animations.

Dashboard Graphic: A graphic that presents multiple metrics, potentially using multiple graphic types, in one consolidated format. (Think of a car's dashboard.)

Design Techniques: Ways of illustrating concepts.

Discriminator: A function, feature, or characteristic that differentiates one product, service, or idea from another.

Dome Graphic: A graphic that looks like a "snow globe" illustrating the containment of elements. The dome graphic is especially good at communicating protection and security.

E

Exploded Diagram: A graphic showing the disassembled parts of an entity or concept placed in a manner that indicates their relative positions when reassembled.

F

Floor Plan: A graphic depicting the layout of a room(s) or level(s) in a building.

Flow Chart: *See* Process Diagram.

Font: A set of text or symbol-based characters.

Funnel Graphic: A graphic metaphor showing the passing of elements through a conduit (the funnel), resulting in the effective allocation, consolidation, or organization of those elements.

G

Gantt Chart: A bar chart representing time and activity used for planning, tracking, and controlling schedules.

Gauge Graphic: A graphic metaphor using readouts and measurement tools to depict data for analysis.

Gear Graphic: A graphic metaphor depicting how parts work together; it often illustrates processes and interoperability.

H

Hierarchy (visual): An aesthetic approach that visually ranks the relative value or importance of content.

Highlighting: Using contrasting colors, shades, sizes, and visual complexity to draw attention to an element in a graphic.

I

Icon: A representational graphic element that is visually analogous with an action, concept, or entity.

Illustration: A visual representation that is used to make the subject more appealing or easier to understand.

Infographic: Any graphic that clarifies or explains. Also called an information graphic.

L

Layout: The way slide elements are positioned and arranged relative to one another and the surrounding space.

Learner Empathy Map (LEM): A mind map technique to capture audience likes, dislikes, and biases.

Learner Motivation Map (LMM): A technique to capture your audience's pains, gains (benefits), and fears.

Learning: The ability to understand, recall, and adopt (apply) what is shared.

Line Chart: A graphic showing the changes in quantitative data using lines, where the position of a line represents the proportional value of the data.

Literal Method: A process for conceptualizing graphics by showing exactly what is described or stated as a way to clarify, explain, or support a claim.

Looping Graphic: A graphic that depicts a repeating process or event.

M

Macro: A set of coded instructions used in Microsoft Office software.

Map Graphic: A graphic showing a region of physical space, such as a continent, country, city, or office building.

Matrix: *See* Table.

Metaphor (visual): A depiction or explanation of an action, concept, or entity that replaces (having the same applicable characteristics as that which is replaced) another action, concept, or entity, making an implicit comparison to improve communication. Essentially, replace one entity or concept for another where the replacement shares the same applicable characteristics.

Mindshare: The awareness of a company, product, service, or idea.

Motivator: The pain, gain, or fear that gives the audience a reason to care about your PowerPoint content and motivates them to learn.

N

Network Diagram: A diagram showing the connections between elements that compose a network.

Noise (visual): Too many visual or textual elements or "busy" textures or imagery on a slide. Visual noise often induces a negative opinion of the subject matter.

O

Ockham's Razor: A widely accepted and proven postulate asserting that simplicity in design is preferred over complexity.

Organizational Chart: A graphic depicting the hierarchy, arrangement, structure, or relationship of a group of elements. (Typically, an organization and its personnel are the subject matter.)

P

Peg Graphic: A graphic showing the interconnectivity of entities or ideas to create a unified whole (think Legos).

Photograph: A picture of a person, place, or thing.

Pie Chart: A graphic that communicates percentages of the whole using proportional segments. Also called a segmented chart.

Pipe Graphic: A graphic metaphor representing the isolated linear flow of elements.

Point Chart: A graphic that shows quantitative data using plotted points.

Presentation Gremlins: Mischievous, unseen bugs that try to sabotage successful PowerPoint presentations. They are defeated by using the process shared in this book.

Presenter: The person, organization, or entity most associated with the PowerPoint presentation. The presenter can be referred to as *trainer, facilitator,* or *educator.*

Process Diagram: A graphic showing the flow or progression of steps in a process or event. Also called a flow chart.

Puzzle Graphic: A graphic metaphor representing the synergy of separate elements that creates a new whole.

Pyramid Graphic: A graphic metaphor that depicts the hierarchy, arrangement, structure, or relationship of a group of elements. The bottom elements support the elements above.

R

Render: The physical creation (in any media) of a slide.

Risk Matrix: A table that depicts varying levels of risk as affected by the influences of one or more variables.

Road Graphic: A graphic metaphor depicting the path between the "as is" or "before" state to the "to be" or "after" state.

S

Scale Graphic: A graphic metaphor that illustrates comparison.

Simile (visual): A depiction or explanation of an action, concept, or entity that augments (having a logical relevance to that which is augmented) another action, concept, or entity, making a comparison to improve communication.

Skeuomorphism: A design aesthetic to render images that resemble their real-word equivalents.

Slide: A single page in a presentation.

Spiral Graphic: A graphic metaphor that illustrates the evolution of an action, concept, or entity through a cyclical process.

Stacked Diagram: A graphic that depicts the hierarchy, arrangement, structure, or relationship of a group of elements. A stacked diagram can also show flow or a progression of steps in a process, similar to a pyramid or process diagram, but it can be more versatile.

Stair Graphic: A graphic metaphor depicting steps in a process.

Step-by-Step Graphic: A graphic that depicts the execution of a linear process.

Storyboard: A sequence of sketches or mock designs with direction and explanation representing a set of slides or presentation.

Symbol: A representational graphic element that has a learned meaning or accepted connotation for an action, concept, or entity.

Symmetry (visual): A graphic can be equally cut in half using a central axis as the dividing line (usually vertically or horizontally divided). The more alike both halves are, the more symmetrical the image.

T

Table: A grid that correlates data along two axes. A lengthier but more descriptive definition is an array of rows and columns (arranged in a grid) interconnecting elements. The point of row and column convergence reveals the data that link the action, concept, or entity indicated in the row title and the column title. Also called a matrix.

Takeaway: Your message. It should include an explicit or implicit motivation.

Target Audience: The person(s) for whom your PowerPoint content was intended.

Template: A file that acts as a blueprint for your slides. Templates often include slide layouts, a color theme, a font theme, an effects theme, background styles, and content.

Theme: A set of attributes that define the appearance of your PowerPoint content. It describes your colors, fonts, effects, and background. Setting up and following your themes makes it easy to change layouts, colors, and fonts.

Thumbnail: A small version of a slide or image.

Timeline: A graphic that linearly represents time.

U

Unconscious Communication: The emotional effects that PowerPoint content and delivery have on your audience.

V

Vee Diagram: A type of process diagram that illustrates the relationships (between the two arms of the *V* shape) and verification path of interoperable elements.

Venn Diagram: A graphic that shows the relationship or synergy of disparate elements through the overlap of those elements.

Visualization: To see the graphic components in your mind's eye before rendering.

W

Waterfall Diagram: A type of process diagram that depicts the linear flow of steps in a progressive nature.

Wonky: Flaky, shaky, or odd.

References

Introduction

Ariely, D. 2010. *Predictably Irrational: The Hidden Forces That Shape Our Decisions.* New York: Harper Perennial.

Bargh, J.A., ed. 2007. *Social Psychology and the Unconscious: The Automaticity of Higher Mental Processes.* New York: Psychology Press.

Dijksterhuis, A. 2009. "The Beautiful Powers of Unconscious Thought." *Science Briefs,* October. www.apa.org /science/about/psa/2009/10/sci-brief.aspx.

Gaskins, R. n.d. "Robert Gaskins Home Page." www.robertgaskins.com/#powerpoint-history.

Gladwell, M. 2005. *Blink: The Power of Thinking Without Thinking.* New York: Little, Brown.

Haidt, J. 2006. *The Happiness Hypothesis: Finding Modern Truth in Ancient Wisdom.* New York: Basic Books.

Kruglinski, S. 2006. "Does Psychotherapy Work?" *Discover,* April: 58-61.

PowerPointInfo. 2017. "PowerPoint Usage and Marketshare." Infogram. https://infogram.com/PowerPoint -usage-and-Marketshare.

Wilson, T.D. 2004. *Strangers to Ourselves: Discovering the Adaptive Unconscious.* Cambridge, MA: Belknap Press.

Chapter 1

Bounds, A. 2007. *The Jelly Effect: How to Make Your Communication Stick.* Chichester, U.K.: Capstone.

Renvoisé, P., and C. Morin. 2005. *Neuromarketing: Is There a "Buy Button" Inside the Brain? Selling to the Old Brain for Instant Success.* San Francisco: SalesBrain Publishing.

Robinson, K. 2006. "Do Schools Kill Creativity?" TED video, 19:22. Feb. www.ted.com/talks/ken_robinson _says_schools_kill_creativity.

Scott, S.J. 2014. *S.M.A.R.T. Goals Made Simple: 10 Steps to Master Your Personal and Career Goals.* Archangel Ink.

Sinek, S. 2008. "How Great Leaders Inspire Action." TED video, 17:58. Sept. www.ted.com/talks/simon_sinek _how_great_leaders_inspire_action.

Taylor, J.B. 2008. "My Stroke of Insight." TED video, 18:35. Feb. www.ted.com/talks/jill_bolte_taylor_s _powerful_stroke_of_insight.

WikiHow. 2016. "How to Learn Any Subject Without Teachers." WikiHow. www.wikihow.com/Learn-Any -Subject-Without-Teachers.

Chapter 2

Deutschman, A. 2007. *Change or Die: The Three Keys to Change at Work and in Life.* New York: HarperCollins.

Kahneman, D., and A. Tversky. 1984. "Choices, Values, and Frames." *American Psychologist* 39(4): 341-350.

Lehrer, J. 2009. *How We Decide.* New York: Houghton Mifflin Harcourt.

Newberg, A., and M.R. Waldman. 2012. *Words Can Change Your Brain: 12 Conversation Strategies to Build Trust, Resolve Conflict, and Increase Intimacy.* New York: Penguin.

Overstreet, H.A. 2003. *Influencing Human Behavior.* Kessinger.

Chapter 3

Bounds, A. 2007. *The Jelly Effect: How to Make Your Communication Stick.* Chichester, UK: Capstone.

Vogel, D.R., G.W. Dickson, and J.A. Lehman. 1986. "Persuasion and the Role of Visual Presentation Support: The UM/3M Study." Working Paper Series, June. MISRC-WP-86-11. Minneapolis: University of Minnesota. http://misrc.umn.edu/workingpapers/fullpapers/1986/8611.pdf.

Chapter 4

Peters, T. 2005. *Design: Innovate, Differentiate, Communicate.* London: DK.

Chapter 5

Burmark, L. 2002. *Visual Literacy: Learn to See, See to Learn.* Alexandria, VA: ASCD.

Embry, D. 1984. "The Persuasive Properties of Color." *Marketing Communications,* October.

Harris, R.L. 1999. *Information Graphics: A Comprehensive Illustrated Reference.* New York: Oxford University Press.

Huggett, C. 2017. *Virtual Training Tools and Templates.* Alexandria, VA: ATD Press.

Johnson, V. 1992. "The Power of Color." *Successful Meetings* 41(7): 87, 90.

Martinez-Conde, S., and S.L. Macknik. 2014. "How the Color Red Influences Our Behavior." *Scientific American,* November 1. www.scientificamerican.com/article/how-the-color-red-influences-our-behavior.

Modern Office Technology. 1989. "Business Papers in Color: Just a Shade Better." *Modern Office Technology* 34(7): 98-102.

Tufte, E.R. 1983. *The Visual Display of Quantitative Information.* Cheshire, CT: Graphics Press.

University of Rochester. 2011. "Color Red Increases the Speed and Strength of Reactions." University of Rochester, June 2. http://rochester.edu/news/show.php?id=3856.

Chapter 6

Gates, B. 2009. "Mosquitos, Malaria and Education." TED video, 20:14. Feb. www.ted.com/talks/bill_gates _unplugged.

McKee, R. 1997. *Story: Substance, Structure, Style, and the Principles of Screenwriting.* New York: HarperCollins.

About the Author

As of publication, Mike is one of 37 Microsoft PowerPoint MVPs in the world. He is a visual communication expert, professional speaker, educator, and award-winning author. He regularly conducts workshops and creates graphics, presentations, and content for companies like Microsoft, Subaru, FedEx, Xerox, Dell, and Boeing, as well as at learning institutions, small organizations, and government agencies.

Mike owns Billion Dollar Graphics (BillionDollarGraphics.com) and 24 Hour Company (24hrco.com), and has also written the book *Do-It-Yourself Billion Dollar Graphics*. Additionally, he created Build-a-Graphic software, which helps you make professional presentations and graphics fast. Contact info@billiondollargraphics.com or visit BillionDollarGraphics.com to learn more.

* * *

With this book, you get 100 professional, editable PowerPoint graphics. Use them to make amazing presentations, infographics, and other learning materials. Study the graphics, break them apart, and look at the animations to learn how to do it yourself. To download your new PowerPoint graphics, go to www.BillionDollarGraphics.com/PowerPoint.

Index

3-D Format and Bevel, 75–77
3-D Rotation, 75–77

A

Ackmann, Heather, 64
Action buttons, 88–89
aesthetic hierarchy, 110–111
Align and Distribute Objects, 78
Altman, Rick, 131
Animation, 85–86
aspect ratio, 81–82
asymmetrical balance, 105
audience
    considerations, 11, 13–14, 26–30
    respecting your, 134–135
audio
    adding, 91
    editing, 92
    Recording, 96–97
    during virtual presentations, 150

B

backup plan, having a, 133–134
balance and symmetry, 104–105
being genuine, 132
benefits
    gain as a motivator, 38–41
    as supporting slides, 43–46
best practices for delivering presentations
    being passionate, 131–132
    being yourself, 132
    engaging learners, 135–139
    having a backup plan, 133–134

practicing out loud, 130–131
respecting your audience, 134–135
testing everything, 133
using a checklist, 133
using a delivery pattern interrupt, 132
writing a script or speaker notes, 130
bevels, 75–76
BMW Financial Services, 23
body language, 146
Bounds, Andy, 20, 50
brand recognition, 69
Bretschneider, Ric, 72
Burmark, Lynell, 100

C

challenges for the audience to encourage
    engagement, 138
Change or Die (Deutschman), 39
Charts, 82–83, 118–123
checking your work, 67
checklist, using a, 133
clarity, 115, 122
classes, online, 33
cognitive curiosity
    cognitive dissonance, 60
    revealing content slowly, 61
    safe surprises, 59–60, 107, 135
colors
    and brand recognition, 69
    choosing, 2–3, 102–103
    the color wheel, 101–102
    cultural considerations, 100–101
    effect on learning and comprehension, 103

emotional reactions to, 100–102

Fill and Line options, 74–75

modifying, 80–81

selecting a professional palette, 103–104

Themes, 70–71

communication

conscious *vs.* unconscious, 4–7

surface, 4

concerns, understanding your audience's, 27

conscious communication, 4–7

continuation, 107

Crop, 91–92

customizing PowerPoint, 72

D

data presentation through quantitative charts, 118–123

default features, 2

Deliver phase, 7–8

best practices for delivering presentations, 130–139

body language, 146

engagement, 37–38, 59–60, 127, 135–139

face-to-face presentations, 143, 144–147

handling questions, 146, 155

hybrid presentations, 143, 154–156

learning from watching other presentations, 129

resolving technical issues, 145, 149

standard view *vs.* Presenter View, 146

virtual presentations, 143, 148–153

word flow, 130

delivery pattern interrupt, using a, 132

Design phase, 7–8

design principles overview, 99–100

determining total slide count, 56–57

key steps, 37

PowerPoint functions, 69–97

professionalism, 67, 106, 125

rendering style, 68–69

safe surprises, 59–60, 107, 135

storyboarding, 37, 49–65, 124–125

takeaway structure, 41–47

understanding learner motivation, 38–41

Deutschman, Alan, 39

Discover, Design, and Deliver phases overview, 7–8

Discover phase, 7–8

audience considerations, 11, 13–14, 26–30

choosing your goals, 20–21

hotel chain example of the Solution Matrix, 18–19

Learner Empathy Map (LEM), 28–30

learning approach, determining the right, 27–30

measuring success, 21–22

planning and data gathering, 15

prioritizing during the, 33

resource assessment, 24–25

Solution Matrix, 17–19, 21

solving the learner's problem, 16–19

subject matter expertise, 31–33

surgery example of observation, 32

technical and procedural requirements, 22–24

variables inside and outside of your control, 14–15

dot density (dpi), 92–93

E

Editing Pictures, Video, and Audio, 91–92

Edit Points, 76

elephant and rider example of the human brain, 6–7, 125

emotional reactions

to colors, 100–101

to fonts, 114–115

to shapes and lines, 108

empathy

Learner Empathy Map (LEM), 28–30

as a tool for understanding your audience, 40

engagement, 37–38, 59–60, 127, 135–139

equipment, checking, 133

evaluating

learning systems, 21–22

your presentation, 139–140

Excel, 83

Exporting and Sharing, 94–95

F

face-to-face presentations
10 strategies for presenting, 144–147
about, 143
fear as a motivator, 38–41
feedback, asking for, 139–140
file types, 94–95
Fill and Line options, 74–75
fonts
serif *vs.* sans serif, 113
size recommendations, 114
to support your message, 115
Format Painter, 82
Format Shape, 74–75, 78

G

gain as a motivator, 38–41
games for reinforcement of skills, 136–137
Gates, Bill, 137–138
goals
choosing realistic learning objectives, 20–21
SMART, 22
validating, 21–22
graphics. *See also* images
creating professional, 7
graphic styles, 68–69
including meaningful, 62–64
infographics, 116–117
photographs, 123–124
quantitative charts, 118–123
skeuomorphism, 68
symbols, 117–118
types of, 64
visual noise, 109–110
vs. graphical elements, 64
grid, using a, 111
Grouping, 96

H

Haidt, Jonathan, 6–7
Haims, Nolan, 42
Handouts view, 152
The Happiness Hypothesis (Haidt), 6–7
harmony and unity, 106–107
Harris, Robert L., 123
hierarchy, 110–111
highlighting patterns, 119–122
honesty, 32
Howell, Tom, 88, 92
humor, 139
hybrid presentations
7 strategies for, 154–156
about, 143
equal involvement for local and virtual learners, 155
Hyperlink, 88

I

idea board for inspiration, 97
images. *See also* graphics
getting a higher-quality company logo, 96
raster, 92–94
vector, 92–94
infographics, 116–117
Information Graphics: A Comprehensive Illustrative Reference (Harris), 123
Insert Picture, Video, and Audio, 91
Interactivity, 88–91

J

The Jelly Effect (Bounds), 20, 50
Johnson, Sandra, 51, 111

L

layers of a slide, 79
layouts
Slide Master, 71–75
using a grid, 111
Learner Empathy Map (LEM), 28–30
Learner Motivation Map (LMM), 29, 40

learning
    approach, determining the right, 27–30
    conscious and unconscious communication, 4–7
    elephant and rider example of the human brain,
        6–7, 125
    online resources, 33
    subject matter expertise, 31–33
lines and shapes, 108
logo, getting a higher-quality, 96

M
margins, 111
McKee, Robert, 136
measuring success, 21–22
Merge Shapes, 79–80
Microsoft Excel, 83
mistakes, recovering after, 132
mobile devices, slide size for, 81–82
Morph transition, 87–88
motivation
    cognitive curiosity, 59–61
    pain, fear, and gain, 38–41

N
needs of training, principal, 3–4
nervous habits, eliminating, 132
Notes Pages, 75, 130

O
Ockham's razor, 51
on-demand training, 152

P
pain as a motivator, 38–41
participation, encouraging, 134–135
pattern interrupt, using a, 132
patterns, highlighting, 119–122
photographs, 123–124
pictures
    adding, 91
    editing, 91

stock visuals, purchasing, 123–124
placeholder text, 64
PowerPoint
    customizing, 72
    three phases of the process, 7–8
    usage statistics, 1
PowerPoint features and functions
    Adding Text and Styles, 81
    Align and Distribute Objects, 78
    Animation, 85–86
    Charts, 82–83
    Color, 80–81
    Editing Pictures, Video, and Audio, 91–92
    Exporting and Sharing, 94–95
    Format Painter, 82
    Grouping, 96
    Insert Picture, Video, and Audio, 91
    Interactivity, 88–91
    interrelated nature of, 69
    Merge Shapes, 79–80
    Notes Pages, 75, 130
    Recording, 96–97, 152
    Reorder Objects, 79
    Resolution, 92–94
    Sections, 74
    Shapes, 74–78
    Slide Master, 71–75
    Slide Size, 81–82
    SmartArt, 83–84
    Themes, 70–71
    Transitions, 86–88
practicing out loud, 130–131
Presenter View, 130, 146
principal needs of training, 3–4
printing considerations, 92–93
problem-solving and the Solution Matrix, 16–19, 21
process diagram symbols, 108
professionalism, 67, 106, 125
proficiency, determining audience, 27
props during a presentation, 137–138
proximity, 107

Q

quantitative charts, 118–123
questions, handling, 146, 155

R

Ramos, Tony, 23, 130
raster images, 92–94
Recording, 96–97, 152
rendering design principles
    balance and symmetry, 104–105
    color, 100–104
    hierarchy, 110–111
    layout (grid), 111
    shapes and lines, 108
    text, 111–115
    unity and harmony, 106–107
    visual noise, 109–110
    visuals, 115–124
    graphic styles, 68–69
    proper construction and layout, 37
Reorder Objects, 79
repetition, 107
requirements
    intake forms, 23
    technical and procedural, 22–24
    understanding, 23
Resolution, 92–94
resources
    assessing your, 24–25
    efficiently using, 37
    stock visuals, video, and audio, 123–124
respecting your audience, 134–135
rewards to encourage engagement, 138–139
rhythm, 107
Rindsberg, Steve, 96
rotation, 76–77

S

safe surprises, 59–60, 107, 135
Sections, 74
Section Zoom, 89–90

Selection Pane, 79
Shapes, 74–78
shapes and lines, 108
Shaw, Glenna, 70, 121
shortcuts
    Chart Elements, 121
    getting the screen to go black, 147
    menu options, 70
    placeholder text, 64
    removing text formatting, 113
    Selection Pane, 79
silence, 130, 132
similarity, 107
simplicity, 115, 122
size of slides, 81–82
skeuomorphism, 68
Slide Master, 71–75
Slide Show, 146
Slide Size, 81–82
Slide Sorter view, 64
Slide Zoom, 89
SmartArt, 83–84
SMART goals, 22
Solution Matrix, 17–19, 21
standard view *vs.* Presenter View, 146
steering wheel example of unconscious activities, 5
step-by-step diagrams, 63
stock visuals, video, and audio resources, 123–124
Story: Substance, Structure, Style, and the Principles of Screenwriting (McKee), 136
storyboarding
    cognitive curiosity, 59–61
    as a fast and agile process, 58–59
    including meaningful graphics, 62–64
    key requirements, 50–51
storyboarding process
    overview, 51–52
    step 1: outline, 52–55
    step 2: conceptualizing and sketching slides, 56–64
    step 3: building a mock design in PowerPoint, 64
    step 4: testing, 65

step 5: updating, 65
structures, 55–56
as a timesaver, 37, 124
total slide count, 56–57
storytelling, 50, 135–136
subject matter expertise, 31–33
Summary Zoom, 89–90
supporting slides, 43–46
surface communication, 4
Swinford, Echo, 52, 109, 122, 132
symbols, 117–118
symmetry and balance, 104–105

T

tabs as visual cues, 56
takeaway(s)
    advantages of an effective, 37–38, 46
    benefit-driven, 45–46
    developing the, 43–46
    as the keystone of your training materials, 37, 124
    multiple levels of, 45–47
    pain, fear, and gain as motivators, 38–41
    statement structure, 41–42
telling a story, 50
templates
    to create harmony, 106
    Slide Master, 71–75
Terberg, Julie, 97, 107, 115
terminology, 3
testing everything before a presentation, 133
text
    adding and styling, 81
    fonts, 113–115
    formatting the text box, 78
    making words the focus of a slide, 111–112
    placeholder, 64
Themes, 70–71
Thomas, Gillian, 68
time considerations
    determining slide count, 56–57
    when developing a presentation, 9

tips
    Action buttons, 89
    adopting change, 39
    Animation Painter, 86
    Apply To All command, 87
    blowouts for complex explanations, 45
    changing spacing around text, 81
    conveying information clearly, 61
    copyright laws, 93
    fear as a motivator, 39
    font size, 114
    Format Painter, 82
    hiring others, 24
    honesty, 32
    keeping your story active, 139
    learner exercises, 59
    placeholder text, 64
    quantitative charts and diagrams, 123
    rendering style, 69
    saving Themes, 72
    SmartArt, 84
    using sections to organize slides, 65
    visual hierarchy, 111
tools. See PowerPoint features and functions
training on demand, 152
traits of an effective presentation, 1
Transitions, 86–88
Tufte, Edward, 122

U

unconscious communication, 4–7, 102–103
unity and harmony, 106–107

V

validating goals, 21–22
variables inside and outside of your control, 14–15
vector images, 92–94
videos
    adding, 91
    editing, 92
virtual presentations

16 strategies for presenting, 148–153
about, 143
webinar tools, 148–149
Visual Literacy: Learn to See, See to Learn (Burmark),
   100
visuals
   tabs as visual cues, 56
   visual noise, 109–110

W

webinar tools, 148–149
white space, 107
Wilson, John, 79, 113
WordArt, 2

X

X, Y, and Z axis rotation, 77

Z

Zoom, 89–91